"Wisdom Journal"

90 Days to Clarity, Calling, and Creative Breakthroughs for Current and Aspiring Writers

DR. CHARIS M. ROOKS

The Kingdom Writer Collection "Wisdom Journal": *90 Days to Clarity, Calling, and Creative Breakthroughs for Current and Aspiring Writers*

Published by: Sapience Atelier Publishing
Publishing Consulting: Sapience Atelier Publishing & Consulting Division
Cover Designer: Sapience Atelier Publishing Cover Art Division in collaboration with Aaftab Shelkh
Typesetting: Cali Pettiford (https://inspiredscribepress.com)
Editor: Sapience Atelier Publishing & Consulting Division (https://www.drcharisrooks.com/sapience-atelier-publishing)
Author Website: (https://www.drcharisrooks.com)

Library of Congress Control Number: 2025921958
ISBN: 979-8-218-88536-6

Printed in the United States of America

Purpose

The Kingdom Writer Collection is a transformative series designed to inspire and empower writers from every literary genre and background. This compilation, filled with invaluable books, products, and resources, seeks to identify your unique voice, activate your God-given potential, and educate and motivate you by offering support and testimonies that resonate with your writing journey in God's Kingdom. Join me on this divine adventure and let your words be the vessel through which God's message is shared, and His Kingdom is expanded. Embrace your calling and discover the impact of the Kingdom Writer Collection, where your writing is not just a pursuit, but a sacred and privileged duty.

-Dr. Charis M. Rooks

Acknowledgement

I dedicate this book to God, my Source, my Sustainer, and my Guide. Without His divine wisdom, grace, and unwavering presence, none of these pages would exist. Every word, every idea, and every breath I take is a testament to His faithfulness in my life.

There were seasons when the weight of my calling felt too heavy, when distractions, doubts, and life's challenges pressed in on every side. In those moments, it was only through prayer, fasting, and surrendering my will that I found the strength to continue. The truth is, without God, I would not have been able to write a single sentence, let alone pick up a pen or pour out my heart onto these pages.

My journey as a writer, mentor, and publisher has not been easy. Building Sapience Atelier, serving fellow writers, and answering the call to inspire others has come with its share of obstacles, financial, emotional, and spiritual. Yet through every trial, God has been my anchor. He opened doors, provided resources, and surrounded me with support, even when I felt alone.

I thank God for every breath, every idea, every opportunity, and every reader who encounters this work. May this book serve as a reflection of His love and a reminder that with Him, all things are possible. To God be all the glory, now and forever.

This Journal Belongs To

What a privilege and honor it is to be the pen in the hand of our creator.

Welcome

Welcome to The Kingdom Writer Collection "Wisdom Journal": 90 Days to Clarity, Calling, and Creative Breakthroughs for Current and Aspiring Writers

Are you just beginning your writing journey, or longing to go deeper in your calling as a faith-driven writer? Writing is more than putting words on a page, it's an act of obedience, healing, and service to God. The path isn't always easy. Distractions, doubts, and difficult seasons are part of the process. I understand, because I've walked through grief, insecurity, and uncertainty myself, both as a writer and as a mentor.

This journal comes from those real experiences. Inside, you'll find spiritual encouragement, practical wisdom, and the same caring mentorship I give in person. Each day, you will discover a Scripture, a reflection, an action step, thoughtful journal questions, and a prayer. My hope is that these pages help you renew your mind, strengthen your sense of who you are, and embrace your special voice as a Kingdom writer.

Let this journal be your friend as you grow, heal, and use your words to make a difference in your community. You are not alone. God is with you and so am I, cheering you on every step of the way.

A Word from My Own Journey

I have walked through many seasons as a writer. Some seasons were full of inspiration and joy. Others were hard, marked by grief, uncertainty, and the heavy weight of life. Losing my mother and my husband changed me deeply, not just as a person, but also as a writer and mentor. In those hard times, I learned that writing is more than just being creative. Writing is a spiritual discipline, a way to draw closer to God and experience His healing in your life. In the quiet moments, when words were hard to find, I felt God's gentle encouragement and His steady presence.

I share this with you because I want you to know you are not alone. The distractions, doubts, and delays you face are real. But so is the calling God has placed on your life. God has given you a special voice and a story that matters. My journey has shown me that every setback, every tear, and every moment of uncertainty can help us grow and find breakthroughs, if we keep showing up and trust God with our writing.

What You'll Find in These Pages

This journal is set up to guide you through 90 days of clarity, calling, and creative breakthroughs. Each day has a special purpose:

1. **Scripture**: Start each day with God's Word. This is the foundation for all Kingdom writing.
2. **Reflection**: Read encouragement and practical wisdom from my own journey and from writers I've mentored.
3. **Journal Questions**: Answer thoughtful prompts that help you dig deeper, face challenges, and learn new things about yourself.
4. **Prayer**: End each day with a prayer, asking God to guide your thoughts, words, and creativity.

5. **Action Step**: Take one simple action to put your faith into practice and build good habits.

I hope you use this journal as a safe and special space where you can be honest and open. Give yourself permission to ask tough questions, celebrate your small wins, and remember that growth doesn't always happen in a straight line. Sometimes, the biggest changes happen quietly, and your faithfulness in this season will bring results in God's perfect timing.

A Call to Kingdom Writers

As a mentor, I have seen how much writers can grow when they give their gifts to God's purpose. No matter if you write fiction, nonfiction, devotionals, letters, or your own story your words can heal, encourage, and inspire others. The world needs your story, and God's Kingdom desires your obedience.

I encourage you to go through these 90 days with an open heart and a willing spirit. Let yourself grow at your own pace. Some days will feel like big breakthroughs. Other days might feel hard or slow. Both are normal and important parts of the journey. If you ever feel stuck, remember that God is always with you, shaping you into the writer He wants you to be.

You are not alone on this path. I am here, cheering for you, praying for your journey, and believing your words will make a difference. Even more, God is with you guiding you, giving you strength, and helping you every step of the way. Let this journal be your companion as you grow, heal, and make a difference with your words. May you find clarity, grow stronger in your calling, and discover new creative ideas. You are a Kingdom writer, called, equipped, and empowered for such a time as this.

With grace and expectation,
Dr. Charis M. Rooks "Doc"

A Prayer for the Journey Ahead

Heavenly Father,

Thank You for every writer holding this journal today. I praise You for the dreams, stories, and callings You have placed in their hearts. As they begin this 90-day journey, please quiet every distraction and calm every anxious thought. Let Your presence cover them, bringing clarity where there is confusion and courage where there is fear.

Lord, I pray that You wake up their creativity and give them a new sense of purpose. Remind them that their words matter, not because of their own strength, but because You have called and equipped them for this special time. Where there is self-doubt, let Your truth speak louder. Where there are hurts, let Your healing flow. Where there is uncertainty, let Your Spirit guide every step.

Give them the discipline to show up each day, even when inspiration feels far away. Fill their minds with wisdom and their hearts with compassion for those who will one day read their words. May this journal become a sacred space, a place to meet You, to grow, and to find breakthrough.

Father, please surround each writer with Your love and protection. Remind them that they are never alone. Show them that You are with them guiding, teaching, and cheering them on. Let their writing become an act of worship, a testimony of Your faithfulness, and a gift that brings light and hope to others.

In Jesus' name I pray, Amen.

Habakkuk 2:2 (NLT)

Then the Lord said to me, "Write my answer plainly on tablets, so that a runner can carry the correct message to others."

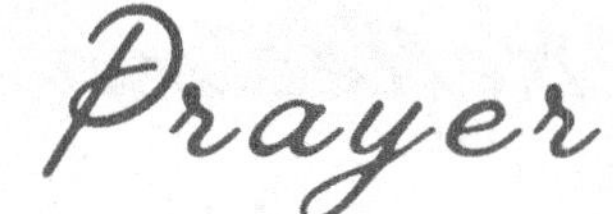

Father, in the name of Jesus,

Thank You for trusting me with a message that matters. Please give me Your wisdom and guidance as I write. Help me let go of anything that hides Your truth, my pride, my fear, or my need for approval. Fill me with Your Spirit so every word I write points others to You. Make my writing a clear path, not an obstacle, for those who are searching for You. Lord, let my words carry Your light and love into every heart that reads them.

Amen.

Action Step

Before you write today, pray for clarity. Then look over your draft and make any hard ideas simpler, so your message is easy to understand and points readers straight to Jesus.

DAY TWO

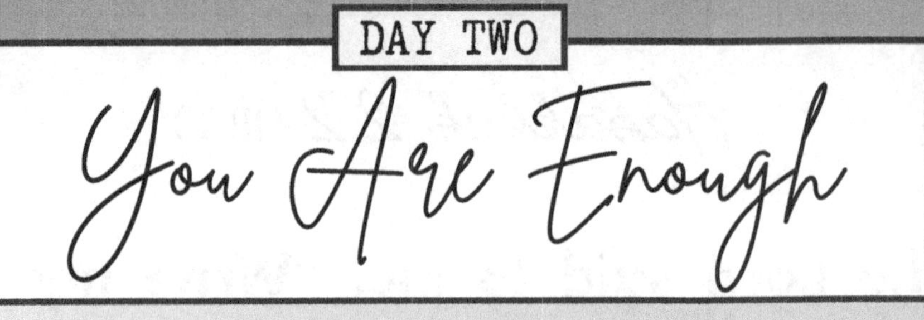

You Are Enough

Philippians 4:13 (NLT)

For I can do everything through Christ, who gives me strength.

Reflection

There will always be voices, inside and outside, that try to tell you that you're not enough. Maybe it's the memory of past mistakes, comparing yourself to others, or the thought that your story doesn't matter. But God's Word is clear: your strength and worth come from Christ alone. Philippians 4:13 isn't just a verse to remember; it's a truth to live by.

God has given you everything you need to write the message He put on your heart. You don't have to have all the answers or be perfect. Your "enough" comes from Him. When doubt tries to sneak in, remind yourself that God's strength shows up best when you feel weak. Your words, when you give them to Him, can heal, inspire, and change lives, not because you're perfect, but because His grace is working through you. Today, let your heart rest in the truth that you are enough, just as you are, because Jesus is more than enough for you.

Date:

Journal Questions

1. **What negative voices do you need to quiet today?**

2. **How can you encourage yourself with God's truth?**

3. **Where do you most need to lean on God's strength in your writing journey?**

Philippians 4:13 (NLT)

For I can do everything through Christ, who gives me strength.

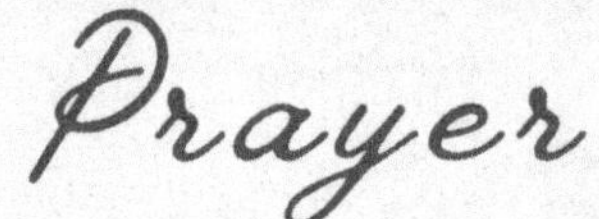

Father, in the name of Jesus,

Thank You that my worth and ability are found in You alone. Please silence every voice that says I'm not enough and fill my mind with Your truth. Give me the courage to write boldly and honestly, knowing You have given me what I need. Fill my heart with Your strength so I can share my words without fear. May everything I write show Your love and point others to how You are enough for all of us.

Amen.

Action Step

Whenever you feel like you're not enough today, pause and say Philippians 4:13 to yourself. Then, write one sentence about how God's grace is helping you on your writing journey.

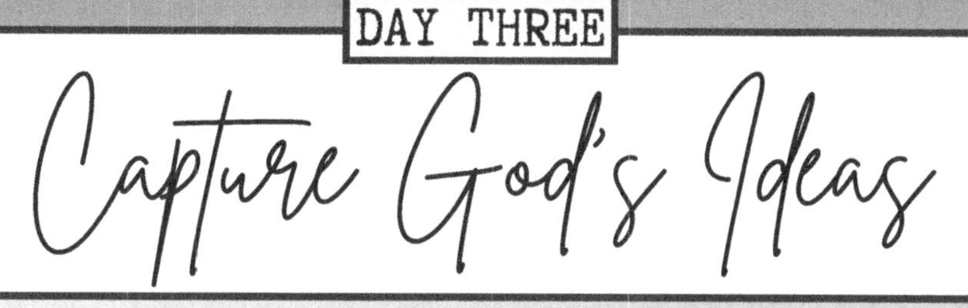

Proverbs 16:3 (NLT)

Commit your actions to the Lord, and your plans will succeed.

Reflection

Some of the most powerful ideas come when we least expect them late at night, in quiet moments, or even during our daily routines. Don't ignore those nudges; God often speaks in the stillness, planting seeds of inspiration that can grow into something life-changing. As writers, we're called to pay attention and be obedient, capturing those divine ideas when they come.

It's easy to brush off a prompting or put off writing it down but remember: obedience in small things opens the door for God to do bigger things. Trust that when you commit your writing and your plans to God, He will guide your steps. Your willingness to care for His inspiration, even when the timing isn't perfect, shows your faithfulness and trust. Keep your journal and your heart open, ready to receive and record every whisper from His Spirit. God is faithful to finish what He starts in you.

Date:

Journal Questions

1. **How do you capture inspiration when it comes?**

2. **Are you committed to following through on God's ideas?**

3. **What practical steps can you take to make sure you don't miss or forget those God-given ideas?**

Proverbs 16:3 (NLT)

Commit your actions to the Lord, and your plans will succeed.

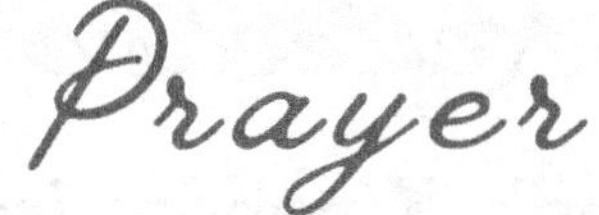

Father, in the name of Jesus,

Thank You for the inspiration You place in my heart, even in unexpected moments. Give me the discipline and awareness to recognize Your voice and the courage to write down what You show me. Help me be faithful with every idea, big or small, and trust that You will finish what You start as I commit my plans to You. Guide my steps and let my writing show Your purpose and glory.

Amen.

Action Step

Keep your journal or a notes app close by today. Whenever you feel a nudge or get a new idea, stop and write it down right away. Trust God to use your obedience in capturing His inspiration.

DAY FOUR

True Leadership Serves

Mark 10:43 (NLT)

But among you it will be different. Whoever wants to be a leader among you must be your servant.

Reflection

True leadership in God's Kingdom isn't about having a title, getting recognition, or being in the spotlight. It's about being willing to serve. Jesus showed servant-leadership in everything He did, and as faith-driven writers, we are called to follow His example. Your influence as a writer isn't measured by how many people know your name, but by how faithfully you point others to Jesus with your words and actions.

When you write with humility, you become someone God can use to touch hearts. Servant-leadership in writing means putting your readers' needs first, offering encouragement, wisdom, and hope, even if no one notices. It means using your platform to lift others up, teach, and inspire, not for your own fame, but to bring glory to God.

Ask yourself: How can I make my writing a ministry of service? Remember, every act of obedience, no matter how small, matters to God. Let your words show Christ's love gentle, humble, and always pointing back to Him.

Date:

Journal Questions

1. **How can you use your platform to serve others?**

2. **What does servant-leadership look like in your writing journey?**

3. **Where might God be inviting you to serve quietly, behind the scenes, through your writing or actions?**

Mark 10:43 (NLT)

But among you it will be different. Whoever wants to be a leader among you must be your servant.

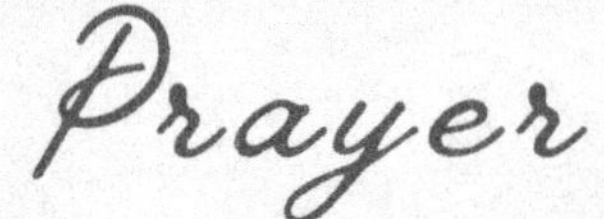

Father, in the name of Jesus,

Teach me to lead by serving others, just as You did. Give me a heart that wants to honor You above everything else. Let my words and actions show Your humility and love and help me use every chance to point others toward You. May my writing be a vessel for Your truth and a source of encouragement for those who need it most.

Amen.

Action Step

Reach out to one reader or fellow writer today with a message of encouragement or support. Put their needs first and practice servant-leadership through a simple, uplifting action.

DAY FIVE

Every Role Matters

1 Corinthians 12:12 (NLT)

The human body has many parts, but the many parts make up one whole body. So it is with the body of Christ.

Reflection

In the body of Christ, every role matters. It's easy to look at what others are doing and feel like your part is too small or doesn't matter, especially when your writing doesn't get the attention you hoped for. But God doesn't measure value by numbers or applause. He looks at faithfulness.

Your calling as a writer is unique. Whether your words reach one person or thousands, they have purpose and power when you give them to God. Don't let comparison or wanting recognition distract you from what God has asked you to do. Stay focused on serving Him with your words, trusting that He sees your faithfulness, even if others do not. Remember, your writing has value, not because of how many people see it, but because God is using it for His glory. Keep your heart anchored in His purpose and let Him decide the impact.

Date:

Journal Questions

1. **In what ways have you compared your calling to others?**

2. **How can you refocus on God's purpose for your writing?**

3. **What steps can you take to celebrate your unique role in the body of Christ, even if it's unseen by many?**

1 Corinthians 12:12 (NLT)

The human body has many parts, but the many parts make up one whole body. So it is with the body of Christ.

Prayer

Father, in the name of Jesus,

Help me value my role in Your kingdom and trust that my writing matters, even when it goes unnoticed. Protect my heart from comparison and the need for recognition. Keep me focused on serving You faithfully, using my gifts for Your glory alone. Remind me that every act of obedience, no matter how small, is precious in Your sight.

Amen.

Action Step

Celebrate your unique part by writing a note to yourself with three ways your words have encouraged or helped someone, even if it was just one person. Put it somewhere you can see it, as a reminder that your writing has value and purpose.

DAY SIX

Rest in Jesus

Matthew 11:28-30 (NLT)

Then Jesus said, "Come to me, all of you who are weary and carry heavy burdens, and I will give you rest. Take my yoke upon you. Let me teach you, because I am humble and gentle at heart, and you will find rest for your souls. For my yoke is easy to bear, and the burden I give you is light."

Reflection

As writers, it's easy to carry more than we should, worries about our words, pressure to perform, and the weight of expectations. Jesus invites us to lay down those extra burdens and come to Him for real rest. When you bring your worries to Jesus, He gives you His peace and swaps your stress for His strength.

Rest isn't just a suggestion; it's a gift and something you need for a healthy writing journey. When you let God refresh your soul, your creativity comes back and your purpose gets clearer. Don't be afraid to pause, breathe, and rest in His presence. You were never meant to do this alone. Let Him carry what you can't and trust Him to renew you for the work ahead.

Date:

Journal Questions

1. **What burdens do you need to lay down today?**

2. **How can you make rest a regular part of your writing routine?**

3. **Where have you been trying to carry things in your own strength instead of trusting Jesus with them?**

Matthew 11:28–30 (NLT)

Then Jesus said, "Come to me, all of you who are weary and carry heavy burdens, and I will give you rest. Take my yoke upon you. Let me teach you, because I am humble and gentle at heart, and you will find rest for your souls. For my yoke is easy to bear, and the burden I give you is light."

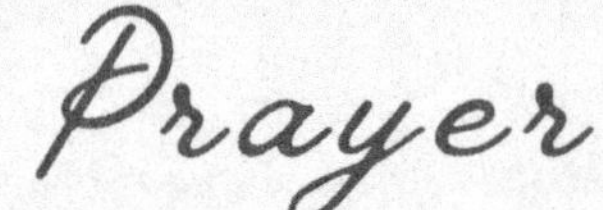

Prayer

Father, in the name of Jesus,

I bring my burdens and worries to You. Teach me to rest in Your presence and trust You with every part of my writing journey. Renew my strength, refresh my spirit, and help me remember that I don't have to carry these loads alone. Let Your peace fill my heart and guide my steps as I write for Your glory.

Amen.

Action Step

Schedule a quiet moment today to pause, pray, and give your writing worries to Jesus. Ask Him to fill you with His peace and renew your creativity before you keep working.

DAY SEVEN

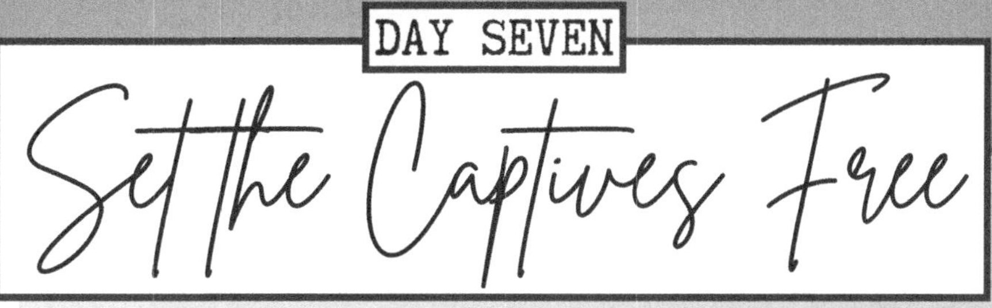

John 8:32 (NLT)

And you will know the truth, and the truth will set you free.

Reflection

Some of the most powerful ideas come when we least expect them late at night, in quiet moments, or even during our daily routines. Don't ignore those nudges; God often speaks in the stillness, planting seeds of inspiration that can grow into something life-changing. As writers, we're called to pay attention and be obedient, capturing those divine ideas when they come.

It's easy to brush off a prompting or put off writing it down but remember: obedience in small things opens the door for God to do bigger things. Trust that when you commit your writing and your plans to God, He will guide your steps. Your willingness to care for His inspiration, even when the timing isn't perfect, shows your faithfulness and trust. Keep your journal and your heart open, ready to receive and record every whisper from His Spirit. God is faithful to finish what He starts in you.

Date:

Journal Questions

1. **Whom might your writing reach that traditional ministry cannot?**

2. **How can you make God's truth plain and easy to understand in your work?**

3. **What fears or hesitations do you need to surrender so you can boldly share the message God has given you?**

John 8:32 (NLT)

And you will know the truth, and the truth will set you free.

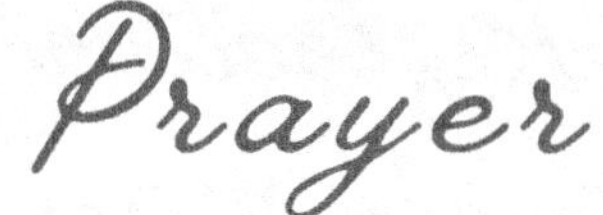

Father, in the name of Jesus,

Let my words be a channel for Your truth and freedom. Give me boldness to share the message You've placed in my heart and use my writing to reach those longing for hope and deliverance. Take away any fear or hesitation and let everything I write be filled with Your Spirit, setting captives free and pointing others to the freedom found in Christ.

Amen.

Action Step

Choose one piece of your writing today and share it publicly on your blog, social media, or with a small group, so your message can reach someone who may never hear it in a traditional ministry setting.

DAY EIGHT

Don't Quit in the Struggle

Galatians 6:9 (NLT)

So let's not get tired of doing what is good. At just the right time we will reap a harvest of blessing if we don't give up.

Reflection

The journey of a Kingdom Writer has both mountaintop moments and valleys of discouragement. There will be days when the words don't come easily, when doubt creeps in, or when progress feels slow. But God's promise is clear: if you keep going and don't give up, you will see the results of your hard work at the right time.

Your perseverance isn't just about finishing a book; it's about honoring the calling God has given you. Every chapter you write, every prayer you pray over your work, and every act of obedience is planting seeds that God will bring to harvest in His perfect timing. Remember, the enemy wants you to quit, but your persistence shows God's faithfulness. Stay motivated by focusing on the purpose behind your writing. Remind yourself that your words have eternal impact, and that God is with you every step of the way. Trust that as you keep going, He will finish what He started in you.

Date:

Journal Questions

1. **What motivates you to keep writing when things get tough?**

2. **How can you encourage yourself to keep going in your writing journey?**

3. **What promises from God can you hold onto when you feel like giving up?**

Galatians 6:9 (NLT)

So let's not get tired of doing what is good. At just the right time we will reap a harvest of blessing if we don't give up.

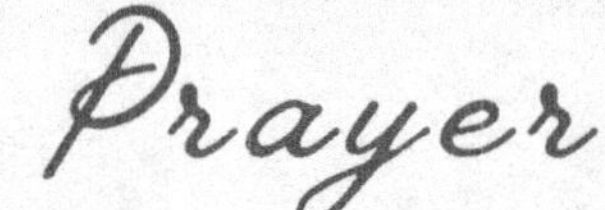

Prayer

Father, in the name of Jesus,

Give me the strength to keep going, even when the journey feels long and hard. Remind me that my work is not wasted and that You will bring a harvest in Your time. Fill me with perseverance, hope, and new passion for the calling You've given me. Help me trust Your timing and keep writing in faith, knowing that You are faithful to finish what You have started.

Amen.

Action Step

Set a small, achievable writing goal for today even if it's just one paragraph. Celebrate your progress as a reminder that perseverance, not perfection, is what leads to a fruitful writing journey.

DAY NINE

God's Plans Are Good

Jeremiah 29:11 (NLT)

"For I know the plans I have for you," says the Lord. "They are plans for good and not for disaster, to give you a future and a hope."

Reflection

God's plans for your life and your writing are always filled with hope. Even when the path ahead feels unclear or progress seems slow, you can be sure that He is guiding every step. God sees more than we do, and His promises never fail.

Sometimes, you might want to control the outcome or worry if your words really matter. But God simply asks you to trust Him, to give Him your plans, your timing, and your fears. Remember, He is faithful to finish what He has started in you. Let your hope be anchored in His Word and remind yourself every day that your future is secure in Him. As you keep writing, lean on His promises and let His direction give you courage for each step.

Date:

Journal Questions

1. **Where do you need to trust God's plans more fully?**

2. **How can you remind yourself of His promises when you feel uncertain?**

3. **What past experiences can you look back on as reminders of God's faithfulness in your journey?**

Jeremiah 29:11 (NLT)

"For I know the plans I have for you," says the Lord. "They are plans for good and not for disaster, to give you a future and a hope."

Prayer

Father, in the name of Jesus,

I trust Your plans for my life and my writing. When I feel uncertain or afraid, remind me of Your promises and fill me with hope and courage for the future. Help me surrender my own desires and expectations, and rest in the truth that You are always working for my good. Guide my steps and let my writing show Your faithfulness.

Amen.

Action Step

Write down one specific hope or dream you have for your writing. Put it somewhere you can see it every day as a reminder to trust God with the outcome and let His promises guide your journey.

DAY TEN

The Struggle Is Real

Romans 7:15 (NLT)

I don't really understand myself, for I want to do what is right, but I don't do it. Instead, I do what I hate.

Reflection

Even Paul, the great apostle and writer of about 24% of the New Testament, faced inner battles and moments of frustration (Romans 7:14-20). He openly admitted his struggles with doing what he knew was right, reminding us that no one is immune to weakness or discouragement. Your struggles do not disqualify you from God's purpose. Instead, they are opportunities to experience His grace in new and deeper ways.

Don't let your battles make you feel unworthy or alone. God understands every challenge you face, and His grace is enough for every step of your journey. When you stumble or feel like you're falling short, remember that God's patience and love are greater than your failures. Lean into His grace, knowing that He is working in you and through you, even in the struggle. Your willingness to keep going, even when it's hard, is a powerful testimony of His strength in your weakness.

Date:

Journal Questions

1. **What struggles do you face in staying obedient to God's call?**

2. **How can you lean on God's grace in your weakness?**

3. **In what areas do you need to give yourself the same grace that God freely gives to you?**

Romans 7:15 (NLT)

I don't really understand myself, for I want to do what is right, but I don't do it. Instead, I do what I hate.

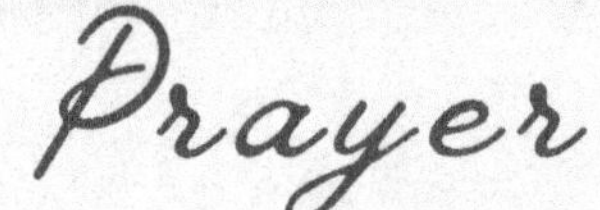

Father, in the name of Jesus,

Thank You for Your patience and grace that cover me in every season. Give me strength to follow Your will, even when it's hard. Help me not to be discouraged by my struggles, but to rely on Your mercy and love. Remind me that Your grace is enough, and that You are faithful to finish the work You have started in me.

Amen.

Action Step

Think about a recent struggle in your writing journey. Write a short note to yourself about how God's grace showed up in that moment. Keep it somewhere you can find it whenever discouragement tries to return.

DAY ELEVEN

You Are God's Letter

2 Corinthians 3:2-3 (NLT)

The only letter of recommendation we need is you yourselves. Your lives are a letter written in our hearts; everyone can read it and recognize our good work among you. Clearly, you are a letter from Christ... written not with pen and ink, but with the Spirit of the living God.

Reflection

You are a living letter, God's message being written and shared with the world through your life and your words. Sometimes, the world tries to confine you, pressuring you to fit its expectations or to hide your true story. But God's purpose for you is bigger than any envelope the world can offer.

Your writing is meant to show the unique message God put inside you, a message that can't be contained by the world's standards. Don't let anyone silence your testimony or quiet your voice. Let the Holy Spirit write through you, making your life and words a testimony that points others to Christ. Break free from the urge to fit in. Embrace your calling as God's letter bold, real, and full of His Spirit. Trust that He is using your story in ways you may never see, reaching hearts and changing lives for His glory.

Date:

Journal Questions

1. **How does your writing reflect the message God wants to share with the world?**

2. **In what ways do you try to fit into the world's expectations, and how can you break free?**

3. **Where do you sense God inviting you to be more real and bold in sharing your story?**

2 Corinthians 3:2-3 (NLT)

The only letter of recommendation we need is you yourselves. Your lives are a letter written in our hearts; everyone can read it and recognize our good work among you. Clearly, you are a letter from Christ... written not with pen and ink, but with the Spirit of the living God.

Prayer

Father, in the name of Jesus,

Let my life and words be a letter that points others to You, written by Your Spirit. Help me break free from the pressure to fit into the world's expectations. Use my story in ways that bring You glory and draw others closer to Your heart. Make my writing a living testimony of Your love, grace, and truth.

Amen.

Find one area where you've been holding back or trying to fit in with your writing. Today, boldly share a piece of your true story, just as you are, without changing yourself to meet others' expectations.

DAY TWELVE

Gracious Words Heal

Proverbs 16:24 (NLT)

Kind words are like honey, sweet to the soul and healthy for the body.

Reflection

Your words have great power, they can bring healing, hope, and strength to those who need it most. Like Barnabas in the early church, you are called to be an encourager, someone who lifts others up and helps them keep going. The world is full of criticism and negativity, but as a Kingdom writer, you have the chance to speak life and healing into every page you write.

Never underestimate the impact of a kind word or a note of encouragement. Sometimes, the simplest message can change someone's day or even their life. Ask God to fill your writing with grace, so that every reader feels seen, valued, and inspired to make a difference. Let your words be a balm for hurting hearts and a spark that brings hope to those who are tired.

Date:

Journal Questions

1. **Who needs encouragement from you today?**

2. **What healing words can you share through your writing?**

3. **How can you be more intentional about using your words to build others up, both in writing and in daily life?**

Proverbs 16:24 (NLT)

Kind words are like honey, sweet to the soul and healthy for the body.

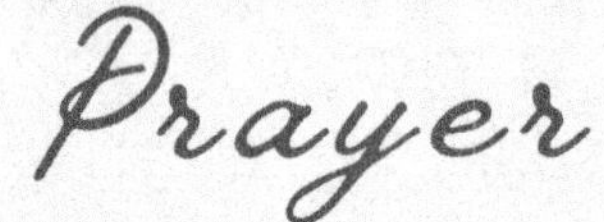

Father, in the name of Jesus,

Fill my words with Your grace and healing. Make me a vessel of encouragement and hope for those who need it. Help me see opportunities to lift others up, and let my writing be a source of strength and inspiration. Use my words to bring comfort, healing, and renewed faith to every heart that reads them.

Amen.

Action Step

Write a short note, message, or comment today to encourage another writer or reader. Use your words to lift up and inspire someone who may need hope or affirmation.

DAY THIRTEEN

God Speaks in Many Ways

Job 33:14 (NLT)

For God speaks again and again, though people do not recognize it.

Reflection

God is always speaking, often in ways we don't expect. Sometimes He whispers through dreams, creative ideas, or gentle nudges in quiet moments. Other times, He may use a conversation, a Scripture, or even a challenge you're facing to get your attention. As a writer, it's important to stay open and pay attention to His voice, trusting that He can use any situation or method to inspire and guide your work.

Don't limit God to speaking only in the ways you're used to. He knows exactly how to reach your heart and guide your writing. Notice those creative sparks, sudden insights, or even the restlessness that makes you seek Him more. Your willingness to listen gives God space to work through your writing in powerful and surprising ways. Stay sensitive, stay ready, and let Him lead you in every part of your life and calling.

Date:

Journal Questions

1. **How has God spoken to you creatively?**

2. **Are you listening for His guidance in all areas of your life?**

3. **What unexpected ways has God used to inspire or redirect your writing journey?**

Job 33:14 (NLT)

For God speaks again and again, though people do not recognize it.

Prayer

Father, in the name of Jesus,

Open my ears and my heart to hear Your voice, however You choose to speak. Help me stay sensitive and ready for Your guidance, especially in my writing. Use dreams, ideas, and quiet moments to direct my steps and inspire my words for Your glory. Let everything I create show Your wisdom and love.

Amen.

Action Step

Set aside a few minutes today to think about your recent experiences. Write down any unexpected ideas, dreams, or moments that felt like gentle nudges, and consider how God might be using them to inspire your writing.

DAY FOURTEEN

Meditate on God's Word

Joshua 1:8 (NLT)

Study this Book of Instruction continually. Meditate on it day and night so you will be sure to obey everything written in it. Only then will you prosper and succeed in all you do.

Reflection

The enemy wants to silence your message by keeping you distracted from God's Word. As a Kingdom Writer, your wisdom, clarity, and strength come from spending time in Scripture. God's Word is your anchor and guide, it shapes your thinking, fuels your creativity, and helps you write with authority and purpose.

Studying and thinking deeply about Scripture isn't just a good habit; it's a lifeline. Make it something you do every day, no matter what. Let God's truth fill your heart and mind, so every word you write is full of His wisdom. When you're rooted in the Word, you can resist discouragement, fight off distractions, and stay focused on your calling. Don't let anything steal your hunger for God's truth. The more you meditate on His promises, the more powerfully He will use your writing to help others.

Date:

Journal Questions

1. **How often do you set aside time to study God's Word?**

2. **What Scripture can you meditate on this week to strengthen your writing?**

3. **How has regular time in Scripture changed your perspective or creativity as a writer?**

Joshua 1:8 (NLT)

Study this Book of Instruction continually. Meditate on it day and night so you will be sure to obey everything written in it. Only then will you prosper and succeed in all you do.

Prayer

Father, in the name of Jesus,

Give me a deep hunger for Your Word. Help me study and meditate on Scripture every day, letting it shape my thoughts, my heart, and every word I write. Let Your truth be my source of wisdom and strength and use my writing to share Your message with clarity and power. Keep me rooted in You and let my work always show Your will.

Amen.

Action Step

Set aside a specific time today to read and think about a passage of Scripture. Then, write a short reflection on how it shapes your view as a Kingdom Writer before you start your next writing session.

DAY FIFTEEN

Ambassadors for Christ

2 Corinthians 5:20 (NLT)

So we are Christ's ambassadors; God is making his appeal through us. We speak for Christ when we plead, "Come back to God!"

Reflection

As a Kingdom writer, you are more than just a storyteller, you are God's representative on earth. Every word you write is a chance to show the beauty, truth, and glory of His kingdom to the world. Your writing can be a window that lets others see Jesus, His love, His compassion, and His hope shining through you.

Being an ambassador means carrying the message and character of Christ wherever you go, including every page you write. Let your writing be marked by grace, honesty, and faith, so anyone who reads your words can encounter more of Jesus. You may never know the full impact of your obedience, but trust that God is using your writing to draw hearts closer to Him.

Date:

Journal Questions

1. **How does your writing represent Christ to others?**

2. **What message do you want to send as His ambassador?**

3. **Where is God inviting you to be more intentional about representing Him through your words?**

2 Corinthians 5:20 (NLT)

So we are Christ's ambassadors; God is making his appeal through us. We speak for Christ when we plead, "Come back to God!"

Prayer

Father, in the name of Jesus,

Help me represent You well in everything I write. Let my words show Your love, truth, and glory. Use my writing to draw others closer to Your heart and reveal Your kingdom to the world. Keep my motives pure and let my life be a living testimony of Your grace.

Amen.

As you write today, choose words and stories that reflect Christ's character, grace, honesty, and hope so your readers can experience His love through every page.

DAY SIXTEEN

The Power of Your Role

1 Corinthians 12:12 (NLT)

The human body has many parts, but the many parts make up one whole body. So it is with the body of Christ.

Reflection

You are a vital part of the body of Christ. Just as the lungs are important to the body, your presence and contribution matter deeply. Through your writing, you reach others with words that teach, comfort, and create connections that make the community of believers stronger. God has given you experiences, insights, and a voice that no one else has.

Embrace your unique role with confidence, knowing your words can bring hope, healing, and encouragement to those who need it most. Don't underestimate your impact, even if your audience seems small. Every act of obedience, every story, devotional, or word of encouragement helps build up the body of Christ and brings glory to God. Use your gifts boldly, trusting that God is using your writing to serve, equip, and inspire His people.

Date:

Journal Questions

1. **How does your writing help or serve others in the body of Christ?**

2. **What unique gifts or perspectives do you bring to your writing ministry?**

3. **How can you intentionally use your writing to build up and unite the community of believers?**

1 Corinthians 12:12 (NLT)

The human body has many parts, but the many parts make up one whole body. So it is with the body of Christ.

Prayer

Father, in the name of Jesus,

Thank You for making me a valuable part of Your body. Show me how to use my gifts to serve and encourage others. Help me embrace my unique role, and let my writing be a source of strength, unity, and hope for the body of Christ. May everything I write, say, and do point back to You and bring You glory.

Amen.

Action Step

Reach out to someone in your community today, through a note, message, or post and use your unique voice to encourage or share insight, trusting your words will strengthen and lift up the body of Christ.

DAY SEVENTEEN

Seeds of Change

Proverbs 18:21 (NLT)

The tongue can bring death or life; those who love to talk will reap the consequences.

Reflection

Your words are like seeds; every sentence you write can take root in someone's heart and bring real change. For people who feel far from God, your writing could be a lifeline of hope and truth. Be intentional about planting words that bring life, encouragement, and healing.

Ask the Holy Spirit to guide your writing so your message plants seeds of faith, restoration, and new possibilities. Remember, you may not see the results right away, but God is faithful to bring growth in His timing. Speak life, sow hope, and trust that your obedience will bear fruit for the Kingdom.

Date:

Journal Questions

1. **What kind of seeds are you planting with your words?**

2. **How can you be more intentional about speaking life?**

3. **Who in your life needs to receive seeds of encouragement or hope from you today?**

Proverbs 18:21 (NLT)

The tongue can bring death or life; those who love to talk will reap the consequences.

Prayer

Father, in the name of Jesus,

Let my words plant seeds of hope and transformation. Guide me to speak life in every situation and use my writing to bring Your love and truth to those who need it most. Help me trust You with the harvest, knowing that You are working through every seed I sow.

Amen.

Action Step

Keep your journal or a notes app close by today. Whenever you feel a nudge or get a new idea, stop and write it down right away. Trust God to use your obedience in capturing His inspiration.

DAY EIGHTEEN

Serve, Not Self

1 Peter 4:10 (NLT)

God has given each of you a gift from his great variety of spiritual gifts. Use them well to serve one another.

Reflection

Writing for God is a calling to serve, not to seek the spotlight. The world may chase after recognition and applause, but your purpose as a Kingdom writer is to be a blessing to inspire, uplift, and encourage others for God's glory. When you write with a heart to serve, your words become a channel of God's grace, reaching those who need hope, wisdom, or comfort.

Ask God to keep your motives pure, so your writing is never about impressing others but always about blessing them. Remember, some of your most powerful and meaningful work may never be widely seen, but it will be deeply valued by those God wants to reach. Let your legacy be one of service, humility, and love.

Date:

Journal Questions

1 **How can you shift your focus from self to service?**

2 **Who can you serve through your writing today?**

3 **What practical steps can you take to keep your motives pure as you follow your writing calling?**

1 Peter 4:10 (NLT)

God has given each of you a gift from his great variety of spiritual gifts. Use them well to serve one another.

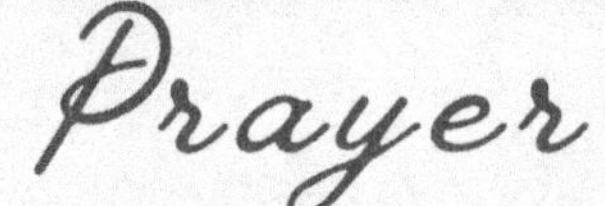

Father, in the name of Jesus,

Help me serve others with my words and keep my motives pure. Remind me every day that my writing is for Your glory and for the good of those You've called me to reach. Let my work be a true reflection of Your love and grace and use me as a vessel to bless and encourage others.

Amen.

Action Step

Pick one reader, friend, or follower today and send them a personal message or share a piece of writing just to encourage and bless them, focus on serving their needs instead of seeking recognition.

DAY NINETEEN

God's Timing, Not Ours

Ecclesiastes 3:1 (NLT)

For everything there is a season, a time for every activity under heaven.

Reflection

We live in a world that celebrates speed, efficiency, and instant results. But God's timing is never rushed and always perfect. As a Kingdom writer, it's easy to feel pressure to finish quickly or publish before you're ready, especially when you see others moving ahead. Remember, God's timing brings peace, fruitfulness, and lasting impact that human effort can't produce.

Waiting on God isn't just sitting still, it's choosing to trust that He sees the bigger picture. When you pause and seek His direction, you invite Him to guide your steps and establish your work. Don't let impatience steal God's best from you. Trust that the season He chooses for your words to be shared will bring the most blessing to you and to those who read your writing.

Date:

Journal Questions

1. **Where have you been impatient in your writing or publishing process?**

2. **How can you tell the difference between your timing and God's timing?**

3. **What practical steps can you take to surrender your timeline and wait for God's direction?**

Ecclesiastes 3:1 (NLT)

For everything there is a season, a time for every activity under heaven.

Father, in the name of Jesus,

Teach me to trust Your timing above my own desires. Give me patience to wait for Your direction and the wisdom to act when You say go. Help me rest in Your perfect plan and trust that You make all things beautiful in Your time.

Amen.

Action Step

Resist the urge to rush your writing process today by taking a deliberate pause. Review your current project, ask yourself if you're moving ahead out of pressure or true readiness, and give yourself permission to wait for God's timing before taking the next step.

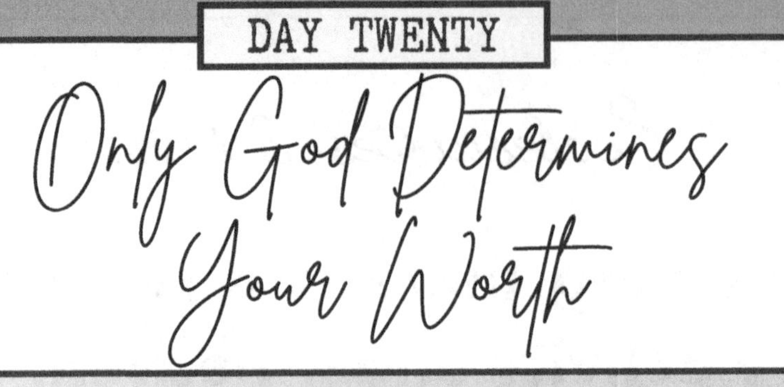

Matthew 18:5 (NLT)

"And anyone who welcomes a little child like this on my behalf is welcoming me."

Reflection

No one can determine your worth but God. The world may try to measure you by achievements, popularity, or approval, but your true value comes from being God's beloved child. You are precious in His sight, chosen and deeply loved, apart from anything you do or accomplish. Let me say this again: you are precious to God, chosen, deeply loved, and valued beyond measure, not for what you do, but simply because you belong to Him.

It's easy to let others' opinions or expectations define you, but God calls you to rest in the identity He has given you. When you receive what God says about you, you can walk confidently in your calling, free from striving for validation. Your worth is secure because it is rooted in His love, not in the shifting standards of others. Embrace this truth and let it shape the way you see yourself and the way you write. You belong to Him, and that is enough.

Date:

Journal Questions

1. **Where do you let others define your value?**

2. **How can you embrace your worth as God's beloved child?**

3. **What truth from God's Word can you declare over yourself today to remind you of your true identity?**

Matthew 18:5 (NLT)

"And anyone who welcomes a little child like this on my behalf is welcoming me."

Prayer

Father, in the name of Jesus,

Help me to receive my worth from You alone. Remind me daily that I am Your beloved child, chosen and valued. Free me from the need for approval and let me rest in Your perfect love.

Amen.

Action Step

Write an affirmation statement about your God-given worth and put it somewhere you'll see it every day. Use it as a reminder to let His love, not others' opinions, define your value and inspire your writing.

DAY TWENTY-ONE

God Guides Your Steps

Proverbs 16:9 (NLT)

We can make our plans, but the Lord determines our steps.

Reflection

Mistakes and detours are a natural part of any journey, but they never catch God off guard. He sees the bigger picture and uses every twist and turn for your growth and His glory. Even when you feel like you've missed it or taken a wrong turn, trust that God is guiding your steps. He has a purpose for you and your writing, and He's working all things together for your good, even the moments you wish you could erase.

Surrender your plans and your setbacks to Him, knowing that nothing is wasted in His hands. Every lesson, every redirection, and every closed door is part of the process that leads you closer to your divine assignment. Trust that as you walk in obedience, God is faithfully leading you, step by step, toward the impact He designed you to make.

Date:

Journal Questions

1. **How has God redirected your path after a mistake or setback?**

2. **What does it look like for you to trust God's guidance in your writing process?**

3. **Where do you need to surrender control and allow God to lead, even if the way forward isn't clear?**

Proverbs 16:9 (NLT)

We can make our plans, but the Lord determines our steps.

Father, in the name of Jesus,

Thank You for ordering my steps, even when I make mistakes. Help me trust Your plan and follow Your leading, knowing You are working all things for my good. Give me faith to surrender my journey to You and courage to keep moving forward, confident that You are guiding me toward my divine assignment.

Amen.

Action Step

Think about a recent mistake or setback in your writing journey. Write down one lesson or positive outcome God has brought from it. Keep it as a reminder that nothing is wasted in His hands.

DAY TWENTY-TWO

Watch for Divine Appointments

Romans 12:4-5 (NLT)

Just as our bodies have many parts and each part has a special function, so it is with Christ's body. We are many parts of one body, and we all belong to each other.

Reflection

You may be the answer to someone's prayer today. Your words have weight and purpose, even when you don't see the full impact. As you keep writing and standing strong in your calling, remember that God uses your faithfulness to encourage, uplift, and strengthen others in the body of Christ.

Never underestimate the power of your obedience. Sometimes a single sentence or a heartfelt story can be just what someone needs to keep going. Stay sensitive to the Holy Spirit's prompting, He may put specific people on your heart who need your words of hope and truth. You are a vital part of the body, and your voice matters. Keep writing, keep standing strong, and trust that God is using you to bless others in ways you may never fully realize.

Date:

Journal Questions

1. **Who has God placed on your heart to encourage through your writing?**

2. **How can you remind yourself of your value to the body of Christ?**

3. **What steps can you take to be more intentional about supporting and uplifting others through your writing?**

Romans 12:4-5 (NLT)

Just as our bodies have many parts and each part has a special function, so it is with Christ's body. We are many parts of one body, and we all belong to each other.

Prayer

Father, in the name of Jesus,

Thank You for making me a vital part of Your body. Use my words to bless, encourage, and strengthen others. Help me see the people You want me to reach and be faithful in sharing hope and truth. Let my writing be a source of unity and encouragement for the body of Christ.

Amen.

Action Step

Reach out to someone who comes to mind today, by sharing a personal story, sending a note, or posting encouragement. Trust that your words may be the answer to a prayer they haven't voiced.

DAY TWENTY-THREE

Renew Your Mind

Romans 12:2 (NLT)

Don't copy the behavior and customs of this world but let God transform you into a new person by changing the way you think. Then you will learn to know God's will for you, which is good and pleasing and perfect.

Reflection

Your thoughts are powerful, they shape not only your writing, but the direction of your entire life. God calls you to look at your thinking and intentionally align it with His Word, not the changing standards of the world. When you make Scripture your foundation, you invite God to transform your perspective, bringing clarity and purpose to your writing journey.

Renewing your mind is a daily process that takes surrender and intention. As you meditate on God's truth, old patterns of fear, doubt, or negativity are replaced with faith, hope, and confidence in His promises. This transformation brings freedom and helps you know God's will—not just for your writing, but for every part of your life. Let His Word shape your mindset, your creativity, and your calling.

Date:

Journal Questions

1. **What thoughts or attitudes do you need to surrender to God for renewal?**

2. **How has God's Word helped transform your thinking in the past?**

3. **What practical steps can you take today to fill your mind with God's truth and reject the world's patterns?**

Romans 12:2 (NLT)

Don't copy the behavior and customs of this world but let God transform you into a new person by changing the way you think. Then you will learn to know God's will for you, which is good and pleasing and perfect.

Prayer

Father, in the name of Jesus,

Renew my mind with Your truth. Help me reject the patterns of this world and embrace Your will for my life and writing. Transform my thoughts, attitudes, and perspective so that everything I create is rooted in Your Word and guided by Your Spirit.

Amen.

Pick one Scripture that speaks to your current mindset and write it at the top of your workspace today. Use it as a reminder to align your thoughts and your writing, with God's truth throughout your day.

DAY TWENTY-FOUR

Be Happy with Your Calling

Colossians 3:23 (NLT)

Work willingly at whatever you do, as though you were working for the Lord rather than for people.

Reflection

Be happy with your calling to write, knowing it's a gift from God and part of His bigger purpose. Writing isn't just about sharing your own thoughts, it's about partnering with God to bring light, encouragement, and truth to others. When you accept your assignment with joy, your words carry a special anointing that can touch lives in ways you may never fully see.

Remember, your writing is an act of worship and service. God delights in your obedience and your willingness to pour out your heart for His glory. Even on days when the work feels hard or goes unnoticed, trust that your faithfulness is making a difference. Celebrate your progress, find joy in the creative process, and keep your focus on serving the Lord through every word you write.

Date:

Journal Questions

1 **How can you find joy in your writing journey today?**

2 **What does it look like to write with all your heart for the Lord?**

3 **In what ways can you remind yourself that your writing is a ministry to others and a gift back to God?**

Colossians 3:23 (NLT)

Work willingly at whatever you do, as though you were working for the Lord rather than for people.

Prayer

Father, in the name of Jesus,

Help me find joy in my calling and write with passion and purpose for You. Remind me that my words matter, not just for me, but for those You want to reach through my writing. Let my work be an offering of worship and a reflection of Your love.

Amen.

Action Step

Take a moment today to celebrate your writing journey, list one recent accomplishment or moment of joy in your work and thank God for the gift and purpose He's given you as a writer.

DAY TWENTY-FIVE

Faith in God's Unstoppable Promises

Genesis 27:33 (NLT)

"Isaac began to tremble uncontrollably and said, 'Then who just served me wild game? I have already eaten it, and I blessed him just before you came. And yes, that blessing must stand!'"

Reflection

After Isaac realized he had given the blessing to Jacob instead of Esau, he didn't take it back. Isaac's faith recognized that God's promises are so strong, they cannot be undone, even when we make mistakes. Isaac had faith, but he still messed up in the flesh. Yet, he trusted that God's purpose would stand.

As a Kingdom writer, you may have moments where you "miss it", where your humanity, emotions, or circumstances lead you to choices you wish you could undo. But faith knows that God is greater than your mistakes. His promises and plans for you are not cancelled by your failures. Like Isaac, you can rest in the assurance that God's blessing is bigger than your mess-ups. Keep moving forward, trusting that even when you fall short, God is still working out His purpose in and through your life.

Date:

Journal Questions

1. **Where have you experienced God's faithfulness even after a mistake?**

2. **How does Isaac's story encourage you to trust God with your writing journey, even when you mess up?**

3. **What promise from God do you need to hold onto today, no matter your circumstances or past choices?**

Genesis 27:33 (NLT)

"Isaac began to tremble uncontrollably and said, 'Then who just served me wild game? I have already eaten it, and I blessed him just before you came. And yes, that blessing must stand!'"

Prayer

Father, in the name of Jesus,

Thank You that Your promises are greater than my mistakes. Help me trust You even when I mess up. Let my faith rest in Your faithfulness and give me courage to keep moving forward as a Kingdom writer. Use my story, including my failures, to bring You glory and encourage others who need hope and a fresh start.

Amen.

Action Step

Think of a recent moment where you felt you "missed it" in your writing or decisions. Write down a statement affirming that God's promises for you remain secure. Use it as motivation to keep moving forward with confidence.

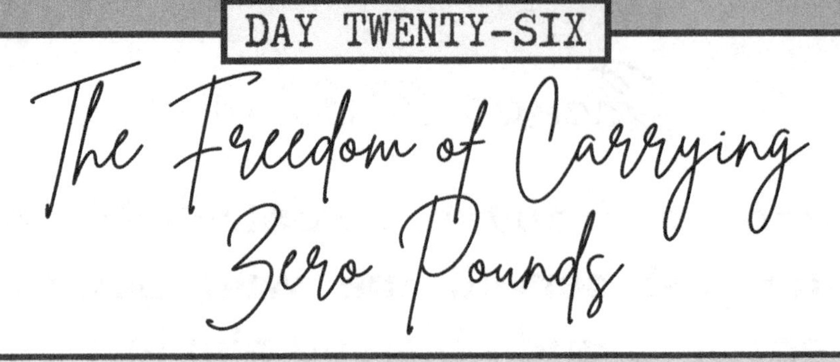

Job 33:14 (NLT)

"For God speaks again and again, though people do not recognize it."

Reflection

As writers, we are called to carry "zero pounds", to live and create free from the weight of hurts and offense. When you hold onto pain, disappointment, or bitterness, your creativity is limited and your spiritual "load limit" is exceeded. God never meant for you to carry burdens He has already offered to bear. Instead, He invites you to travel light, letting go of every offense and trusting Him to heal and restore you.

Letting go of hurts isn't just for your own peace, but for the sake of your calling. When you write from a place of freedom, your words have more power to heal, encourage, and inspire others. God often speaks in moments when your heart is unburdened through gentle whispers, creative ideas, or sudden clarity. Don't let unresolved pain block your ability to hear His voice or hold back your message. Choose forgiveness, release the weight, and make room for God's presence and inspiration to flow through you.

Date:

Journal Questions

1. **What hurts or offenses are you still carrying that may be weighing down your writing journey?**

2. **How might releasing these burdens free you to hear God's voice more clearly?**

3. **What practical steps can you take today to forgive, let go, and travel light as a Kingdom writer?**

Job 33:14 (NLT)

"For God speaks again and again, though people do not recognize it."

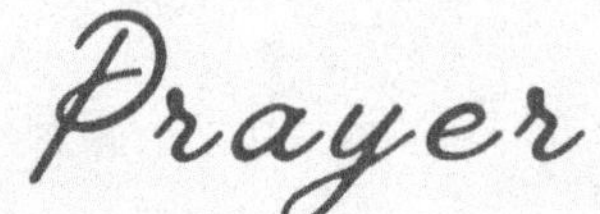

Father, in the name of Jesus,

Help me to carry zero pounds, releasing every hurt and offense into Your hands. Free my heart from burdens You never intended me to bear. Fill me with Your peace and help me hear Your voice, so my writing can flow from a place of freedom and grace. Let my words bring healing and hope to others, just as You have done for me.

Amen.

Action Step

Take a moment today to identify any lingering hurt or offense and intentionally release it. Write down what you're letting go of, then tear up or discard the note as a symbolic act of traveling light and making room for God's inspiration.

DAY TWENTY-SEVEN

Avoid Complaining

Philippians 2:14-15 (NLT)

"Do everything without complaining and arguing, so that no one can criticize you. Live clean, innocent lives as children of God, shining like bright lights in a world full of crooked and perverse people."

Reflection

Complaining about your writing journey, whether it's about the process, the pace, or your progress, can actually block the grace God has given you for your calling. When you grumble or focus on what's not working, you close your heart to encouragement, inspiration, and the fresh perspective God wants to bring. Complaining makes obstacles look bigger and can blind you to the blessings and opportunities already in front of you.

Instead, choose gratitude and faith. Thank God for every step, even the hard ones, and trust that He is working in you and through you. When you guard your heart against negativity, you make space for God's grace to empower your creativity and perseverance. Remember, your attitude shapes your experience and your message. Let your words, spoken and written, reflect hope, trust, and a willingness to partner with God for His glory.

Date:

Journal Questions

1. **In what areas of your writing have you found yourself complaining or grumbling?**

2. **How might gratitude and faith shift your perspective and open you to God's grace?**

3. **What practical step can you take today to replace complaints with thanksgiving in your writing journey?**

Philippians 2:14-15 (NLT)

"Do everything without complaining and arguing, so that no one can criticize you. Live clean, innocent lives as children of God, shining like bright lights in a world full of crooked and perverse people."

Father, in the name of Jesus,

Forgive me for the times I've complained about my writing or doubted Your grace. Help me guard my words and attitude, choosing gratitude and trust instead. Fill me with Your perspective, and let my writing journey be marked by faith, hope, and a thankful heart. Use my words to encourage others and bring glory to Your name.

Amen.

Action Step

If you catch yourself starting to complain about your writing today, intentionally replace each complaint with a statement of gratitude. Write down at least one thing you're thankful for in your journey to shift your focus toward faith and encouragement.

DAY TWENTY-EIGHT

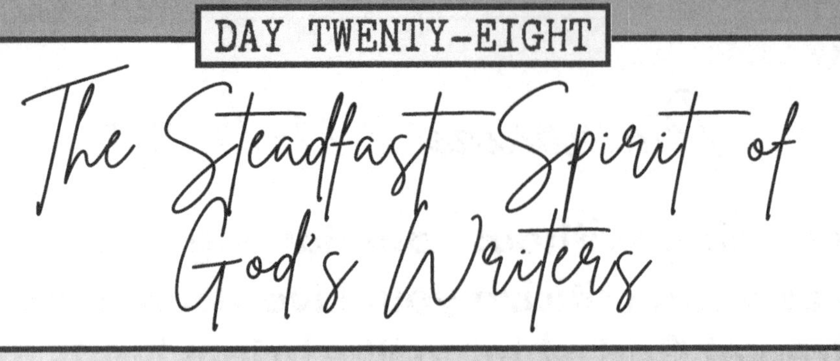

1 Corinthians 3:9 (NLT)

"For we are both God's workers. And you are God's field. You are God's building."

Reflection

God's writers are called to be co-laborers with the Lord, faithful workers who show up, put pen to paper, and trust God to do the rest. This calling isn't about seeking special attention or worrying about results. It's about having a steady spirit, knowing you're partnering with God every time you write.

You don't need to be nervous or wait for perfect conditions. Like a diligent worker arriving for their shift, you can approach your writing with confidence, knowing God is right there with you. The fruit comes not from striving or stressing, but from consistency, faithfulness, and a willingness to "go to work" with the Lord. Your part is to show up; God's part is to bring the increase.

Let your writing routine be marked by trust, peace, and quiet confidence. Release the pressure to make it extraordinary, just be faithful in your assignment and let God handle the outcomes.

Date:

Journal Questions

1. **How does seeing yourself as a co-laborer with God change your approach to writing?**

2. **In what ways can you simplify your writing process and just "go to work" without overthinking?**

3. **Where do you need to let go of anxiety or perfectionism and simply trust God as you write?**

1 Corinthians 3:9 (NLT)

"For we are both God's workers. And you are God's field. You are God's building."

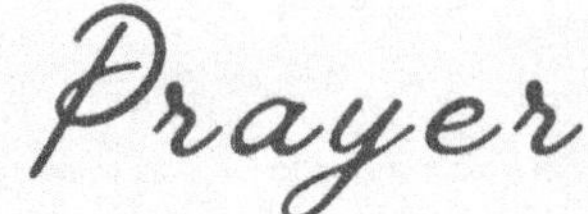

Father, in the name of Jesus,

Thank You for inviting me to be Your co-laborer. Help me approach my writing with a steady, peaceful spirit, free from anxiety or striving. Remind me that my job is to show up and write, and Your job is to bring the increase. Let my faithfulness honor You and use my words for Your glory.

Amen.

Action Step

Set up a simple, consistent writing routine this week. Commit to showing up at a set time each day, focusing on faithfulness rather than results, and trust God to bring the increase through your steady work.

DAY TWENTY-NINE

Listen and Obey

James 1:22 (NLT)

"But don't just listen to God's word. You must do what it says. Otherwise, you are only fooling yourselves."

Reflection

To truly walk with God, you must be willing to listen and obey. Sometimes, God's instruction is clear, He tells you to write the book, share your story, or start the project that's been stirring in your heart. The call isn't just to hear, but to act. Obedience is where faith comes alive and where God's purposes are fulfilled through you.

Delaying or doubting God's prompting keeps you from experiencing the fullness of His blessing and the impact He wants to make through your life. When God says, "Write the book," don't wait for perfect conditions or more confirmation, just obey. Your willingness to follow His voice, even when it stretches you, opens the door for Him to move in ways you never imagined. Let your writing journey be marked by a heart that listens and a spirit that obeys. Trust that as you take each step in faith, God will guide, equip, and use your obedience to bless others and bring Him glory.

Date:

Journal Questions

1. **What has God clearly asked you to do in your writing journey that you've hesitated to obey?**

2. **What fears or excuses have kept you from acting on God's instructions?**

3. **What is one step you can take today to move from hearing to doing, especially if God is telling you to "write the book"?**

James 1:22 (NLT)

"But don't just listen to God's word. You must do what it says. Otherwise, you are only fooling yourselves."

Prayer

Father, in the name of Jesus,

Give me a heart that listens and a will that obeys. When You say, "Write the book," help me move forward in faith and obedience. Remove every fear, doubt, or excuse that holds me back. Let my writing be an act of surrender and trust and use my obedience to accomplish Your purpose in and through me.

Amen.

Action Step

Take immediate action on a writing prompt or project God has placed on your heart. Set aside time today to start, even if it's just outlining your ideas or writing the first paragraph, to show your willingness to listen and obey.

DAY THIRTY

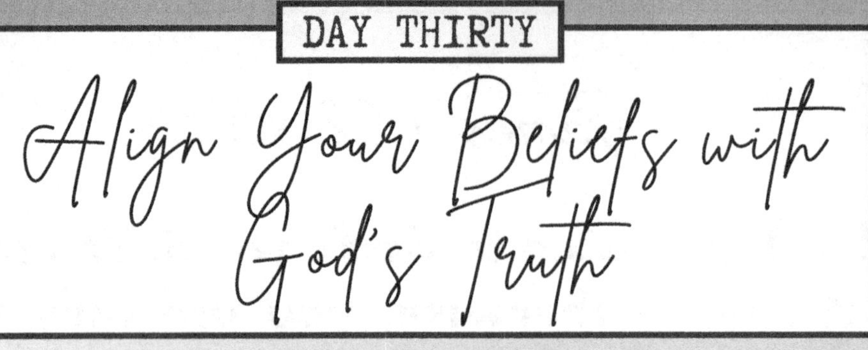

Align Your Beliefs with God's Truth

John 8:32 (NLT)

"And you will know the truth, and the truth will set you free."

Reflection

If your thoughts, beliefs, or opinions about your writing journey aren't lined up with God's Word, you might be believing a lie. The enemy often tries to plant doubts like, "You're not good enough," "God can't use you," or "Your story doesn't matter." None of these are from God. His truth always brings freedom, purpose, and encouragement.

Take time to look at what you believe about your calling as a writer. Are your thoughts rooted in God's promises, or shaped by fear, comparison, or past disappointments? Sometimes, the opinions you hold about yourself are just lies that need to be replaced with God's perspective. When you align your beliefs with His truth, you'll find new confidence, clarity, and passion for your assignment. Let God's Word be the standard for every thought and decision. If you find a lie, replace it with the truth of who God says you are and what He's called you to do.

Date:

Journal Questions

1. **What thoughts or opinions about your writing might be out of alignment with God's truth?**

2. **How can you identify and replace lies with God's promises regarding your calling?**

3. **What truth from Scripture do you need to declare over your writing journey today?**

John 8:32 (NLT)

"And you will know the truth, and the truth will set you free."

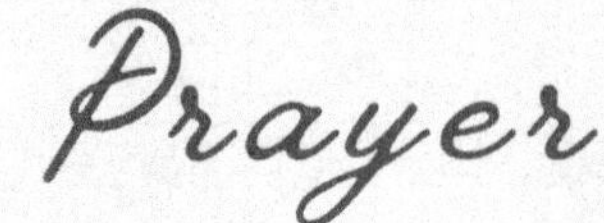

Father, in the name of Jesus,

Show me any lies I've believed about my call to write. Help me align my thoughts and beliefs with Your Word and truth. Give me discernment to know what is from You and what is not. Fill my heart with confidence in Your calling and purpose for my life. Let my writing be a reflection of Your truth and a testimony to Your faithfulness.

Amen.

Action Step

Identify one negative belief or doubt you've had about your writing. Replace it today by writing out a Scripture or truth from God's Word that affirms your calling. Keep it visible as a reminder to align your thoughts with His perspective.

DAY THIRTY-ONE

Greater Is He

1 John 4:4 (NLT)

"You, dear children, are from God and have overcome them, because the one who is in you is greater than the one who is in the world."

Reflection

Never believe that the enemy has more power than God or more influence over your calling. The Spirit of God within you is greater than any obstacle, opposition, or discouragement you may face on your writing journey. There will be moments when fear, doubt, or criticism try to make you feel like you're not equipped or strong enough. But the truth is, you are never alone, God's power is at work in you, helping you stand strong and move forward.

As God's writer, you are not defined by the challenges you face, but by the victory that Christ has already won for you. Stand firm, knowing you are equipped and empowered to overcome every challenge. Let this confidence fuel your creativity and perseverance and remind yourself daily that God's calling on your life is unstoppable when you rely on His strength.

Date:

Journal Questions

1. **Where have you felt intimidated or discouraged in your writing journey?**

2. **How can you remind yourself daily that God's power in you is greater than any obstacle?**

3. **What practical steps can you take to walk in the confidence and authority God has given you as a writer?**

1 John 4:4 (NLT)

"You, dear children, are from God and have overcome them, because the one who is in you is greater than the one who is in the world."

Prayer

Father, in the name of Jesus,

Thank You that Your Spirit in me is greater than any force in the world. Strengthen my faith and remind me every day that I am an overcomer in Christ. Help me stand firm in Your truth, reject fear and discouragement, and walk boldly in the calling You have placed on my life.

Amen.

Write a bold affirmation at the top of today's draft: "God's power in me is greater than any opposition." Then choose one concrete task to complete with that confidence.

DAY THIRTY-TWO

You Are Made New

2 Corinthians 5:17 (NLT)

"This means that anyone who belongs to Christ has become a new person. The old life is gone; a new life has begun!"

Reflection

The enemy wants you to believe that you haven't really changed, that your past mistakes, failures, or old labels still define you. But God's truth is greater: you are a new creation in Christ. Every day is a fresh start, a new chance to walk in the freedom and confidence that comes from your new identity. Mistakes and setbacks do not disqualify you from your calling; they are simply reminders of your need for God's grace.

Let go of the old labels, regrets, and self-doubt that try to hold you back. God's forgiveness is complete, and His mercies are new every morning. As a writer, you have the privilege to share your journey of transformation with others, offering hope that change is possible through Christ. Embrace your new identity and write from a place of victory, not defeat.

Date:

Journal Questions

1. **What old labels or mistakes do you need to let go of today?**

2. **How can you embrace your new identity in Christ as a writer?**

3. **In what ways can you use your story of transformation to inspire others who feel stuck in their past?**

2 Corinthians 5:17 (NLT)

"This means that anyone who belongs to Christ has become a new person. The old life is gone; a new life has begun!"

Prayer

Father, in the name of Jesus,

Thank You for making me new. Help me leave the past behind and walk boldly in my new identity in Christ. Remind me daily that I am forgiven, redeemed, and equipped for every good work. Let my writing show the freedom and hope I have found in You and use my story to encourage others to embrace their new life as well.

Amen.

Action Step

Identify one old label or limiting belief that's been holding you back. Write a replacement truth ("In Christ, I am a new creation") and place it where you'll see it before you write today.

DAY THIRTY-THREE

Your Place Is Irreplaceable

Romans 12:6 (NLT)

"In his grace, God has given us different gifts for doing certain things well..."

Reflection

Your place in the body of Christ is intentional, never random or replaceable. God has given you a writing assignment that is uniquely yours, crafted for your voice, your story, and your season. No one else can fulfill the exact role He's entrusted to you. When you accept this truth, you realize your contribution matters deeply, even if it feels small or unseen.

It's easy to compare yourself to others or wonder if your words make a difference. But God's design is purposeful. Your testimony, your perspective, and your obedience are woven with intention into His bigger plan. If you hold back or try to imitate someone else, there's a gap only you can fill. Your writing may be the answer to someone's prayer, the encouragement for a weary soul, or the spark that ignites new faith.

Step into your assignment with confidence, knowing you are irreplaceable in God's story. Be bold, be faithful, and trust that your obedience has eternal impact.

Date:

Journal Questions

1. **Where have you doubted the value of your unique assignment as a writer?**

2. **What makes your writing and perspective irreplaceable in the body of Christ?**

3. **How can you honor your role and step into it more fully, trusting God's intentional design?**

Romans 12:6 (NLT)

"In his grace, God has given us different gifts for doing certain things well..."

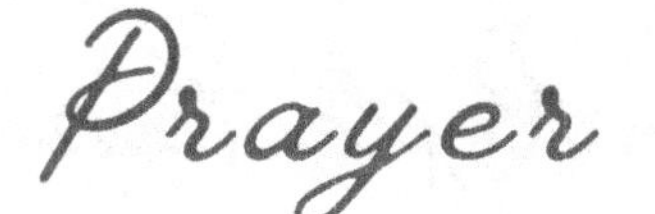

Father, in the name of Jesus,

Thank You that my place in Your body is intentional and irreplaceable. Help me value the assignment You've given me and step into it with faith and boldness. Let my writing fulfill its unique purpose, bringing strength and unity to the body of Christ and glory to Your name.

Amen.

Action Step

Write a short mission statement for your unique assignment (2-3 sentences) and pin it where you draft. Commit to one action today that only you can do in your voice.

DAY THIRTY-FOUR

Let God's Word Guide Every Situation

Psalm 119:105 (NLT)

"Your word is a lamp to guide my feet and a light for my path."

Reflection

In every situation, especially as you write, pause and ask yourself, "What does God's Word say about this?" God's Word is your ultimate source of wisdom and clarity. When you're unsure, discouraged, or facing a decision in your writing journey, let Scripture be your first and final authority. His Word brings light where there is confusion and peace where there is anxiety.

As a Kingdom writer, your words carry more weight and impact when they are rooted in the truth of Scripture. Instead of leaning on your own understanding or the latest trends, let God's Word shape your perspective, your message, and your motives. When you invite the Holy Spirit to speak through the Word, you'll find guidance, encouragement, and inspiration for every step. Make it a habit to bring every challenge, idea, and goal before God, seeking His direction in everything you do.

Date:

Journal Questions

1. **When was the last time you paused to ask, "What does God's Word say about this?" in your writing process?**

2. **How can you make Scripture the foundation for your creative decisions and direction?**

3. **What specific verse or passage could you meditate on today to guide your next step?**

Psalm 119:105 (NLT)

"Your word is a lamp to guide my feet and a light for my path."

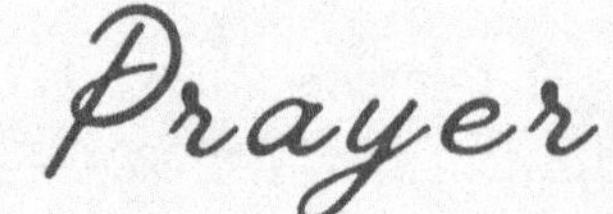

Father, in the name of Jesus,

Help me seek Your Word in every situation, especially as I write. Let Your truth be my guide and my foundation. Remind me to pause and ask for Your perspective and give me a heart that delights in Your instruction. Use Your Word to shape my thoughts, my words, and my journey as a Kingdom writer.

Amen.

Action Step

Before writing today, look up one Scripture that speaks to your current decision or challenge. Note it at the top of your draft and let it guide your next paragraph.

DAY THIRTY-FIVE

Multiply What God Has Given You

Matthew 25:14-30 (NLT)

"The Kingdom of Heaven can be illustrated by the story of a man going on a long trip... He gave five bags of silver to one, two bags of silver to another, and one bag of silver to the last... The servant who received the five bags began to invest the money and earned five more... But the servant who received the one bag dug a hole in the ground and hid the master's money... 'Well done, my good and faithful servant. You have been faithful in handling this small amount, so now I will give you many more responsibilities. Let's celebrate together!'"

Reflection

The parable of the talents teaches us a powerful lesson about stewardship and faithfulness. When God gives you the talent to write, He expects you to use it, multiply it, and invest it for His kingdom, not to hide it or let it go unused. The servant who buried his talent lost even the little he had, while those who invested and multiplied what was given were celebrated and trusted with more.

As a Kingdom Writer, you have been given a unique gift, a book, a message, a ministry. God's desire is that you don't hold back or let fear, comparison, or procrastination keep you from multiplying what He's given you. Faithfulness isn't about quantity or perfection; it's about using what you have, right where you are, and trusting God to bring the increase.

Don't let your writing gift sit dormant. Be diligent, courageous, and creative in how you steward your calling. As you invest your words, your story, and your ministry, God will use your faithfulness to impact lives and expand His kingdom.

Date:

Journal Questions

1. **In what ways have you multiplied or buried the writing talent God has given you?**

2. **What fears or excuses have kept you from investing your gift more fully?**

3. **What practical step can you take this week to multiply your writing ministry for God's glory?**

Matthew 25:14-30 (NLT)

"The Kingdom of Heaven can be illustrated by the story of a man going on a long trip... He gave five bags of silver to one, two bags of silver to another, and one bag of silver to the last... The servant who received the five bags began to invest the money and earned five more... But the servant who received the one bag dug a hole in the ground and hid the master's money... 'Well done, my good and faithful servant. You have been faithful in handling this small amount, so now I will give you many more responsibilities. Let's celebrate together!'"

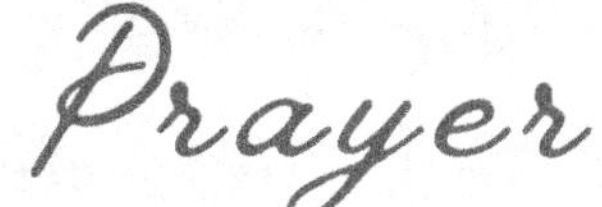

Father, in the name of Jesus,

Thank You for the gift and calling to write. Help me be a faithful steward of what You've entrusted to me. Give me courage to multiply my talent, invest my words, and use my writing for Your kingdom. Remove every fear or excuse that holds me back and let my faithfulness bring You glory and blessing to others.

Amen.

List three concrete ways to "invest" your writing gift today and complete at least one before the day ends.

DAY THIRTY-SIX

Writer's Actions and Motives

Proverbs 16:2 (NLT)

"People may be pure in their own eyes, but the Lord examines their motives."

Reflection

When we write for God, understanding our actions and motives is really important. Every writer has reasons behind what they do, and these reasons help shape their work. God cares deeply about both the words we share and the heart from which they flow.

As you reflect on your writing, ask yourself: Am I writing to impress, to vent, or to genuinely serve and uplift others? Honest self-examination allows your work to be more authentic and impactful. Let God shape your motives, so your actions as a writer align with His purposes and bring Him glory.

Date:

Journal Questions

1. **What motivates you to write, and how do your motives influence your message?**

2. **In what ways can you invite God to examine and purify your motives as a writer?**

3. **How have your actions and intentions shaped the impact of your writing so far?**

Proverbs 16:2 (NLT)

"People may be pure in their own eyes, but the Lord examines their motives."

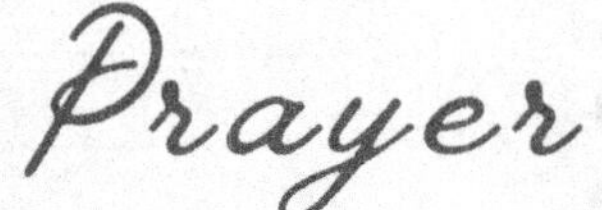

Father, in the name of Jesus,

Search my heart and reveal my true motives as I write. Purify my intentions so that my actions and words reflect Your love and purpose. Help me create with honesty, humility, and faithfulness, so my writing brings encouragement and points others to You.

Amen.

Action Step

Do a quick motives check before writing. Write down why you're drafting today (impress, vent, or serve), then rewrite it into a service-centered intention and proceed with your session.

DAY THIRTY-SEVEN

God's Call Is Greater Than Disability or Fear

Matthew 6:24 (NLT)

"No one can serve two masters. For you will hate one and love the other; you will be devoted to one and despise the other. You cannot serve God and be enslaved to money."

Reflection

This word is for every Kingdom Writer who is physically disabled or who has "disabled" themselves out of fear. Maybe you face real physical limitations, or maybe fear, discouragement, or anxiety has convinced you that you can't move forward. I want you to know: your story and your obedience matter deeply to God and to others who need hope.

There are countless people, some disabled, some not, waiting to see what God can do through someone willing to trust Him, even with limitations. Your willingness to write, to share your journey, and to obey God's prompting is a testimony that faith is greater than fear and that God's power is made perfect in weakness.

If you've stopped writing out of fear, maybe afraid that success would change your circumstances, or worried about losing a safety net like a disability check, bring that fear honestly before God. Ask Him for wisdom, courage, and creative solutions. Remember, you cannot serve both fear and faith or let money be your master. God is your provider, and He is able to open doors, provide resources, and sustain you beyond what you can see.

Don't let physical limitations or fear keep you from your calling. God's grace is enough for you. Your words, written in faith, can inspire, heal, and set others free.

Date:

Journal Questions

1. **In what ways have you let physical limitations or fear "disable" your writing journey?**

2. **What would it look like to trust God with your fears and step out in obedience, even with limitations?**

3. **Who might be encouraged or set free by seeing your faith in action?**

Matthew 6:24 (NLT)

"No one can serve two masters. For you will hate one and love the other; you will be devoted to one and despise the other. You cannot serve God and be enslaved to money."

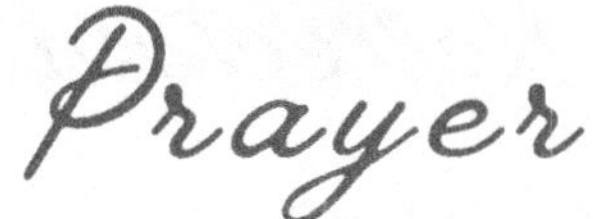

Father, in the name of Jesus,

I surrender my fears, limitations, and excuses to You. Remind me that Your call is greater than my disability or my fear. Give me courage to write and obey, trusting You to provide and make a way. Use my story to encourage others and to show Your power in my weakness. Let my life and my words bring hope, freedom, and glory to Your name.

Amen.

Action Step

Identify one fear or limitation holding you back. Take a small, concrete step today (like writing 100 words or recording a 2-minute voice note) to move forward despite it, proving faith over fear.

DAY THIRTY-EIGHT

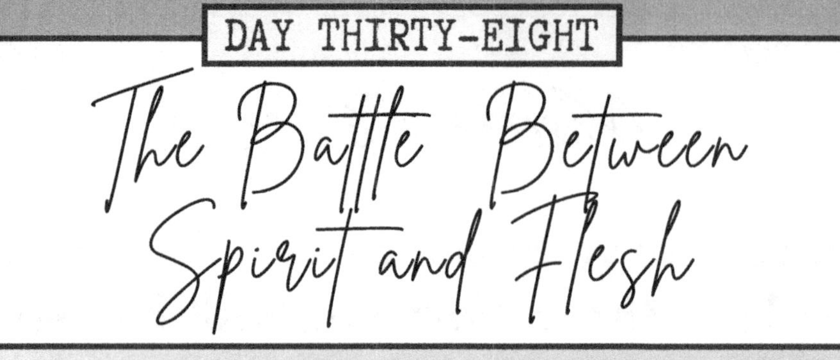

The Battle Between Spirit and Flesh

Romans 7:15 (NLT)

"I don't really understand myself, for I want to do what is right, but I don't do it. Instead, I do what I hate."

Reflection

Every Kingdom Writer knows the tension between spirit and flesh. Deep down, your spirit wants to follow God's will, obey His promptings, and pursue your calling with passion and faith. Yet your flesh, your fears, doubts, and comfort often resists, pulling you the other way.

This inner battle isn't a sign of failure; it's part of the journey. Even Paul, one of the greatest apostles, admitted he struggled to do what he knew was right. The good news is that God understands our weakness and gives us His grace and Spirit to help us overcome. The key is daily surrender: inviting the Holy Spirit to strengthen your spirit, renew your mind, and empower you to choose obedience over comfort.

When you feel the tug-of-war between what God is calling you to do and what your flesh wants, remember that victory comes not by your strength, but by God's. Keep showing up, keep surrendering, and trust that God will help you walk in His will, one step at a time.

Date:

Journal Questions

1. **Where do you feel the tension between your spirit and your flesh in your writing journey?**

2. **What practical steps can you take to feed your spirit and quiet your flesh?**

3. **How has God helped you in the past to overcome the resistance of your flesh and obey His call?**

Romans 7:15 (NLT)

"I don't really understand myself, for I want to do what is right, but I don't do it. Instead, I do what I hate."

Prayer

Father, in the name of Jesus,

Thank You for giving me a spirit that wants to do Your will. Help me recognize when my flesh is resisting Your call and give me strength to choose obedience. Fill me with Your Spirit, renew my mind, and let my life and writing reflect Your heart and purpose.

Amen.

Action Step

When resistance hits today, set a 10-minute timer and just start, no overthinking. Write until the timer ends, then decide your next small step.

DAY THIRTY-NINE

Watch Your Words

Proverbs 18:21 (NLT)

"The tongue can bring death or life; those who love to talk will reap the consequences."

Reflection

Your words carry tremendous power. Every sentence you speak or write has the potential to build up or tear down, to bring hope or discouragement. The enemy wants to twist your words, sowing seeds of doubt or negativity, but when you choose to speak life, you reflect the very heart of God.

As a Kingdom writer, your words are a tool for healing, encouragement, and truth. Be intentional about using your voice to uplift others, whether in conversation, on the page, or in prayer. Ask God to help you guard your tongue, so your words always align with His purpose. Remember, your writing can be a source of blessing and transformation for those who read it. Let your legacy be one of life-giving words that point others to Christ.

Date:

Journal Questions

1. **How have your words impacted others lately?**

2. **What can you do to ensure your words bring life?**

3. **In what situations do you need God's help to speak life instead of reacting in frustration or fear?**

Proverbs 18:21 (NLT)

"The tongue can bring death or life; those who love to talk will reap the consequences."

Prayer

Father, in the name of Jesus,

Let my words be filled with Your life and truth. Guard my tongue and use my writing to bless, encourage, and build others up. Help me speak life even in challenging moments and let everything I say and write reflect Your heart.

Amen.

Action Step

Choose one interaction today (comment, message, or conversation) and deliberately speak or write a life-giving response that encourages and uplifts.

DAY FORTY

As You Think, So You Are

Proverbs 23:7 (NLT)

"For as he thinks in his heart, so is he."

Reflection

Your words and actions are a direct reflection of what you truly believe in your heart. If you want your writing to overflow with God's truth, it starts by letting Him shape your inner beliefs. The world tries to fill your heart with doubt, fear, or insecurity, but God's promises are the foundation for a life and a message full of purpose and power.

Fill your heart daily with His truth. Meditate on His Word, declare His promises over your life, and invite Him to renew your mind. As your beliefs align more closely with God's truth, your words will naturally become a source of encouragement, wisdom, and life for others. Let your writing be the fruit of a heart that is rooted in God's love and anchored in His promises.

Date:

Journal Questions

1 **What beliefs are shaping your words and actions right now?**

2 **How can you fill your heart with God's truth each day?**

3 **In what areas do you need to invite God to reshape your thinking, so your writing reflects His truth?**

Proverbs 23:7 (NLT)

"For as he thinks in his heart, so is he."

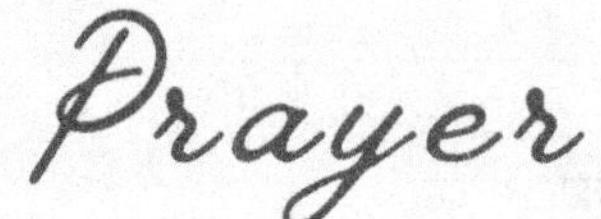

Father, in the name of Jesus,

Shape my heart and thoughts according to Your Word. Let my beliefs align with Your truth so my words and actions reflect Your love, wisdom, and purpose. Fill me daily with Your promises and let my writing overflow with life and encouragement for others.

Amen.

Action Step

Choose one promise from Scripture today. Write it on a card or sticky note and keep it visible while you write to help align your words with that truth.

DAY FORTY-ONE

The Discipline of Listening

Ecclesiastes 5:2 (NLT)

"Don't make rash promises, and don't be hasty in bringing matters before God. After all, God is in heaven, and you are here on earth. So let your words be few."

Reflection

As writers, words are our natural currency. For some of us, myself included, as my grandmother used to say, "You have the gift of gab", it can be especially hard to be quiet. Yet, in our relationship with God, listening is just as important, if not more important, than speaking. God is in heaven; we are on earth. We don't have His perspective, His lenses, or the full picture He sees for our lives and our writing.

It takes humility to pause, quiet your thoughts, and truly listen for God's voice before you rush to fill the silence with your own words, ideas, or plans. The discipline of listening opens your heart to receive divine wisdom, direction, and creativity that you could never find on your own. When you make space to listen, you invite God to shape your message and your journey in ways that far surpass what you could imagine.

Let your writing process be marked by moments of stillness, where you listen for God's whisper and trust that what He wants to say is more important than anything you could say to Him. Your greatest breakthroughs and most powerful words will often come from what you receive in the quiet.

Date:

Journal Questions

1. **When was the last time you paused to listen for God's voice before you started writing?**

2. **What distractions or habits keep you from being still and attentive to God?**

3. **How can you create more intentional space to listen for God's direction in your writing journey?**

Ecclesiastes 5:2 (NLT)

"Don't make rash promises, and don't be hasty in bringing matters before God. After all, God is in heaven, and you are here on earth. So let your words be few."

Prayer

Father, in the name of Jesus,

Teach me to listen more than I speak. Quiet my heart and help me to be still before You. Remind me that Your wisdom and perspective are greater than my own. Let my writing flow from what I receive in Your presence and help me trust that Your voice will guide me every step of the way.

Amen.

Action Step

Schedule a short listening block today (5–10 minutes). Sit in silence, note any insights you sense, and let one guide your next paragraph.

DAY FORTY-TWO

The Value of Your Words

Proverbs 23:7 (NLT)

"For as he thinks in his heart, so is he."

Reflection

Your words and actions are a direct reflection of what you truly believe in your heart. If you want your writing to overflow with God's truth, it starts by letting Him shape your inner beliefs. The world will try to fill your heart with doubt, fear, or insecurity, but God's promises are the foundation for a life and a message full of purpose and power.

Fill your heart daily with His truth. Meditate on His Word, declare His promises over your life, and invite Him to renew your mind. As your beliefs align more closely with God's truth, your words will naturally become a source of encouragement, wisdom, and life for others. Let your writing be the fruit of a heart rooted in God's love and anchored in His promises.

Date:

Journal Questions

1 **What beliefs are shaping your words and actions right now?**

2 **How can you fill your heart with God's truth each day?**

3 **In what areas do you need to invite God to reshape your thinking so your writing reflects His truth?**

Proverbs 23:7 (NLT)

"For as he thinks in his heart, so is he."

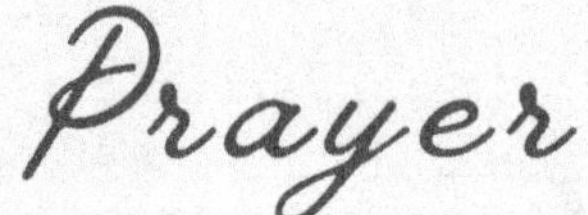

Father, in the name of Jesus,

Shape my heart and thoughts according to Your Word. Let my beliefs align with Your truth so my words and actions reflect Your love, wisdom, and purpose. Fill me daily with Your promises and let my writing overflow with life and encouragement for others.

Amen.

Action Step

Select one promise from Scripture and speak it aloud before writing. Then, draft a paragraph that reflects that truth in your own words.

DAY FORTY-THREE

You Are Someone's Answer

Romans 12:4-5 (NLT)

"Just as our bodies have many parts and each part has a special function, so it is with Christ's body. We are many parts of one body, and we all belong to each other."

Reflection

You may be the answer to someone's prayer today. Your words carry weight and purpose, even when you don't see the full impact. As you keep writing and standing strong in your calling, remember that God uses your faithfulness to encourage, uplift, and strengthen others in the body of Christ.

Never underestimate the power of your obedience, sometimes a single sentence or a heartfelt story can be just what someone needs to keep going. Stay sensitive to the Holy Spirit's prompting; He may put specific people on your heart who need your words of hope and truth. You are a vital part of the body, and your voice matters. Keep writing, keep standing strong, and trust that God is using you to bless others in ways you may never fully realize.

Date:

Journal Questions

1. **Who has God placed on your heart to encourage through your writing?**

2. **How can you remind yourself of your value to the body of Christ?**

3. **What steps can you take to be more intentional about supporting and uplifting others through your writing?**

Romans 12:4-5 (NLT)

"Just as our bodies have many parts and each part has a special function, so it is with Christ's body. We are many parts of one body, and we all belong to each other."

Prayer

Father, in the name of Jesus,

Thank You for making me a vital part of Your body. Use my words to bless, encourage, and strengthen others. Help me see the people You want me to reach and be faithful in sharing hope and truth. Let my writing be a source of unity and encouragement for the body of Christ.

Amen.

Ask God to highlight one person today. Then send them a brief, encouraging message or share a short piece of your writing to uplift them.

DAY FORTY-FOUR

Lose The Lone Wolf Mentality

Ecclesiastes 4:9-10 (NLT)

"Two people are better off than one, for they can help each other succeed. If one person falls, the other can reach out and help. But someone who falls alone is in real trouble."

Reflection

The "lone wolf" mentality is not sustainable for Kingdom writers. While writing is often a solitary act, expanding God's kingdom is never meant to be a solo mission. It's easy to think you have to do this alone, especially when you spend hours writing in isolation. But even Jesus, the greatest leader and teacher, surrounded Himself with disciples. He sent them out in teams, not as lone wolves.

When you try to carry the entire load yourself, you risk burnout, discouragement, and missing out on the richness that comes from collaboration. God designed the body of Christ to work in unity, like a symphony, where each musician plays a unique part, but together they create a beautiful sound. As a Kingdom writer, you are called to stay filled individually, but also to unite with other writers for encouragement, accountability, and shared vision.

Don't let pride, fear, or insecurity keep you isolated. Seek out community, share your journey, and invite others to walk with you. Remember, your words are powerful, but together with others, your impact multiplies, and the kingdom expands in ways you could never accomplish alone.

Date:

Journal Questions

1. **Where have you tried to "go it alone" in your writing journey, and how has that affected you?**

2. **Who are the fellow writers or believers you could invite into your creative process or ministry?**

3. **What practical step can you take this week to build unity and collaboration with others in your writing life?**

Ecclesiastes 4:9-10 (NLT)

"Two people are better off than one, for they can help each other succeed. If one person falls, the other can reach out and help. But someone who falls alone is in real trouble."

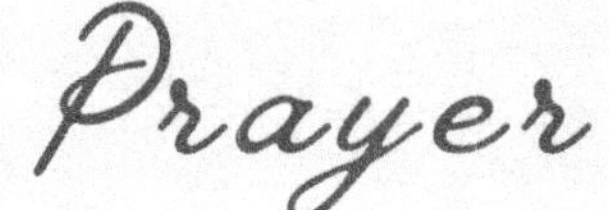

Father, in the name of Jesus,

Help me let go of the lone wolf mentality. Remind me that I am called to community and unity, not isolation. Bring the right people into my life to encourage, challenge, and partner with me as I follow Your call as a writer. Let my words join with others to create a symphony of hope, truth, and transformation for Your kingdom.

Amen.

Action Step

Join or start a small writers' check-in today, message 1–2 peers to share goals for the week and set a brief accountability touchpoint.

DAY FORTY-FIVE

You Are Not an Accident

Ephesians 2:10 (NLT)

"For we are God's masterpiece. He has created us anew in Christ Jesus, so we can do the good things he planned for us long ago."

Reflection

Accidents are the result of human error, not God's design. God doesn't make mistakes, especially when it comes to creating you and giving you your call to write. Your existence, your gifts, and your purpose are intentional. God has uniquely crafted you with a story, a voice, and a mission that no one else can fulfill.

When you doubt your worth or question your assignment, remember that you are not an afterthought or a random occurrence. You are God's masterpiece, created with care and purpose. Your calling to write is not accidental; it's a deliberate part of His plan to reach, encourage, and inspire others. Trust that every detail of your journey has meaning, even when you don't see the full picture yet.

Embrace your identity and your calling with confidence. God's intentionality in creating you means your words matter, your story matters, and your obedience will bear fruit for His kingdom.

Date:

Journal Questions

1. **In what ways have you doubted your purpose or seen yourself as an "accident" in your writing journey?**

2. **How does knowing you are intentionally created by God change your perspective on your calling?**

3. **What step can you take today to embrace your assignment as a Kingdom writer with confidence and gratitude?**

Ephesians 2:10 (NLT)

"For we are God's masterpiece. He has created us anew in Christ Jesus, so we can do the good things he planned for us long ago."

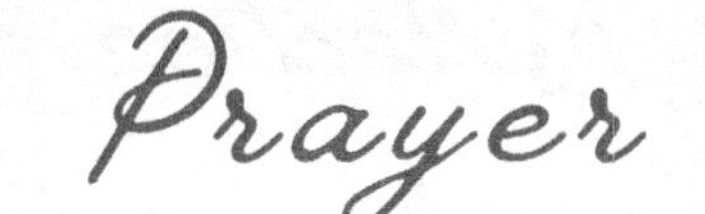

Father, in the name of Jesus,

Thank You that I am not an accident. Remind me that You created me on purpose and assigned my calling with intention. Help me embrace my identity and my writing assignment with confidence, knowing that every part of my journey is in Your hands. Use my words to fulfill Your purpose and bring You glory.

Amen.

Action Step

Write a one-sentence affirmation of God's intentional design for you ("I am chosen by God on purpose for this assignment") and place it at the top of today's draft.

DAY FORTY-SIX

The Importance of Saying Yes to Your Calling

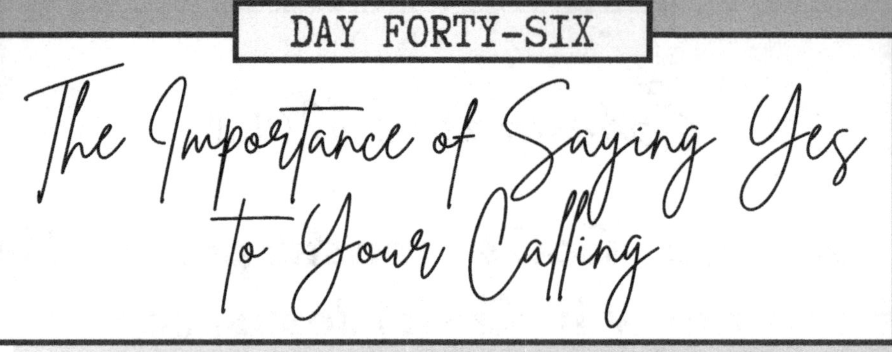

Proverbs 16:24 (NLT)

"Kind words are like honey — sweet to the soul and healthy for the body."

Reflection

Here's a perspective I received from a professor in Bible college that has stayed with me: "When you don't do what God asks you to do, then someone else like me, who says yes, will have to do your job and also my own call. I don't mind helping you out, but I don't want to do what God created you to do while also doing what I was created to do on a long-term basis."

As Kingdom writers, your unique voice and assignment matter deeply. God has entrusted you with a purpose and a message that only you can deliver. When you say "yes" to your calling, you bring healing, encouragement, and strength to others. But when you hold back or hesitate, it places a burden on others and leaves a gap in the body of Christ. Your obedience isn't just about you, it's about the people waiting for the hope, truth, and grace God wants to share through you.

Let your writing be an act of faithfulness and partnership with God. Ask Him to fill your words with grace, so you build up others and fulfill your unique part in His plan. Remember, your "yes" matters more than you know.

Date:

Journal Questions

1. **Where have you hesitated to say "yes" to God's call in your writing?**

2. **How might your obedience encourage or relieve someone else in the body of Christ?**

3. **What specific step can you take today to embrace your unique assignment?**

Proverbs 16:24 (NLT)

"Kind words are like honey — sweet to the soul and healthy for the body."

Prayer

Father, in the name of Jesus,

Help me to say "yes" to what You've called me to do. Fill my words with grace and healing, and let me fulfill my assignment with faithfulness and joy. Don't let me miss the opportunity to be a blessing to others or to leave a gap in Your body. Use my obedience to bring hope, comfort, and restoration wherever You send me.

Amen.

Action Step

Say "yes" today by completing one concrete task only you can do (for example, draft 200 words of your unique message), closing the gap only your voice can fill.

DAY FORTY-SEVEN

Stepping Out in Faith

Hebrews 11:1 (NLT)

"Faith shows the reality of what we hope for; it is the evidence of things we cannot see."

Reflection

Faith is the foundation of your writing journey. There will be times when the path ahead is unclear, when you're unsure if your words will make a difference, or when the outcome seems out of reach. Yet, faith means trusting that God is working through your obedience, even when you can't see the full picture.

Your willingness to write, to share your story, and to follow God's leading, even in uncertainty, is a powerful act of faith. Remember, God honors every step you take in obedience. He sees your heart, your efforts, and your desire to serve Him through your writing.

Trust that He is weaving together every word for His purpose and glory. Let your faith anchor you, knowing that God's faithfulness never fails. Keep showing up, your obedience today is part of a bigger story He is faithfully unfolding.

Date:

Journal Questions

1. Where do you need to step out in faith as a writer?

2. How can you remind yourself of God's faithfulness today?

3. What practical steps can you take to strengthen your faith in this season of your writing journey?

Hebrews 11:1 (NLT)

"Faith shows the reality of what we hope for; it is the evidence of things we cannot see."

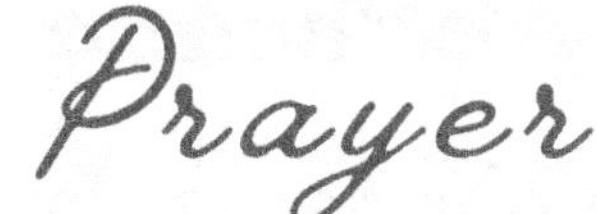

Father, in the name of Jesus,

Help me trust You with my writing, even when I can't see the full picture. Strengthen my faith and remind me daily of Your faithfulness. Give me courage to step out in obedience, knowing You are working through every word I write. Let my journey be rooted in faith, hope, and trust in Your perfect plan.

Amen.

Draft one paragraph today, even if you feel uncertain. Trust God with the outcome and mark it complete as your act of faith.

DAY FORTY-EIGHT

The Blessing of Obedience

Deuteronomy 28:2 (NLT)

"All these blessings will come on you and accompany you if you obey the Lord your God."

Reflection

God's blessings follow obedience. Every "yes" you give Him, whether it's stepping out in faith to share your story, revising a chapter when prompted, or simply showing up to write when it's hard, plants seeds that will bear fruit in due season. Obedience in your writing isn't always easy, and sometimes you may not see the results right away, but trust that God honors every act of surrender.

Often, it's in the small, hidden moments of obedience that the greatest blessings unfold. God sees your willingness to follow His lead, even when it stretches you or feels inconvenient. He promises that as you continue to say "yes" to Him, His favor and provision will follow.

Stay expectant, your obedience is making a way for blessings you can't yet imagine. Keep showing up, trusting that each step of surrender is positioning you for fruit you'll reap in the right season.

Date:

Journal Questions

1. **How has obedience in your writing brought unexpected blessings?**

2. **Where is God asking for your "yes" today?**

3. **What small step of obedience can you take this week to honor God with your writing?**

Deuteronomy 28:2 (NLT)

"All these blessings will come on you and accompany you if you obey the Lord your God."

Prayer

Father, in the name of Jesus,

Help me obey You in every area of my writing life. Give me a willing heart to say "yes" to Your promptings, even when it's uncomfortable or unclear. Remind me that every act of obedience is precious to You and will bear fruit in Your perfect timing. Let my writing journey be marked by surrender, trust, and the blessings that come from following Your lead.

Amen.

Action Step

Choose one small act of obedience today (for example, revise a paragraph you've avoided or share a short excerpt) and complete it, trusting God to multiply the seed you plant.

DAY FORTY-NINE

The Gift of Community

Ecclesiastes 4:9-10 (NLT)

"Two people are better off than one, for they can help each other succeed. If one person falls, the other can reach out and help. But someone who falls alone is in real trouble."

Reflection

Writing can sometimes feel like a solitary journey, but God never intended for you to walk it alone. He designed us for community, people who encourage, challenge, and walk alongside us. There's power in connecting with other writers who understand the highs and lows of the creative process. They can offer fresh perspective, accountability, and the kind of support that helps you keep going when you feel stuck or discouraged.

Don't hesitate to reach out and build relationships with fellow writers. Share your struggles and victories and be willing to lift up others in their journey as well. When you give and receive encouragement, you reflect God's heart for unity and growth.

Remember, your words can bless others, but so can your presence and support in their lives. We're better together, let's build each other up as we pursue God's calling.

Date:

Journal Questions

1. **Who encourages you in your writing?**

2. **How can you support another writer this week?**

3. **What steps can you take to intentionally build or strengthen your writing community?**

Ecclesiastes 4:9-10 (NLT)

"Two people are better off than one, for they can help each other succeed. If one person falls, the other can reach out and help. But someone who falls alone is in real trouble."

Prayer

Father, in the name of Jesus,

Thank You for the gift of community. Help me give and receive encouragement as I walk this writing journey. Show me how to support others and open my heart to the support I need as well. May our connections bring You glory and help us all grow stronger in our calling.

Amen.

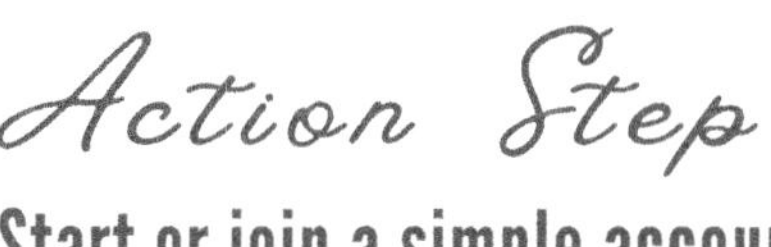

Action Step

Start or join a simple accountability thread today with 1–2 writers. Share your goal for the week and set a quick check-in time.

DAY FIFTY

Purpose Over Perfection

2 Corinthians 12:9(NLT)

"But he said to me, 'My grace is all you need. My power works best in weakness.' So now I am glad to boast about my weaknesses, so that the power of Christ can work through me."

Reflection

God isn't looking for perfection, He's looking for willingness. It's easy to let perfectionism hold you back, making you feel like your work isn't good enough or that you have to have it all together before moving forward. But God's strength shines brightest through your weaknesses and imperfections. He loves to use ordinary people to do extraordinary things, simply because they are willing to say "yes" to His call.

Don't let chasing perfection keep you from fulfilling your purpose. Shift your focus from trying to impress to simply being faithful. Trust that God can use every flaw, every mistake, and every shortcoming for His glory.

When you surrender your imperfections to Him, you make room for His power to work through you in ways you could never imagine. Keep showing up with what you have, and let God do what only He can do through your willing "yes."

Date:

Journal Questions

1. **Where have you let perfectionism hold you back?**

2. **How can you shift your focus to purpose over perfection?**

3. **In what area of your writing do you sense God inviting you to trust Him with your weaknesses?**

2 Corinthians 12:9 (NLT)

"But he said to me, 'My grace is all you need. My power works best in weakness.' So now I am glad to boast about my weaknesses, so that the power of Christ can work through me."

Prayer

Father, in the name of Jesus,

Use my imperfections for Your glory. Help me let go of perfectionism and focus on Your purpose for my life and my writing. Remind me that Your grace is sufficient and Your strength is made perfect in my weakness. Let my willingness be my offering and use every part of me, flaws and all, to point others to You.

Amen.

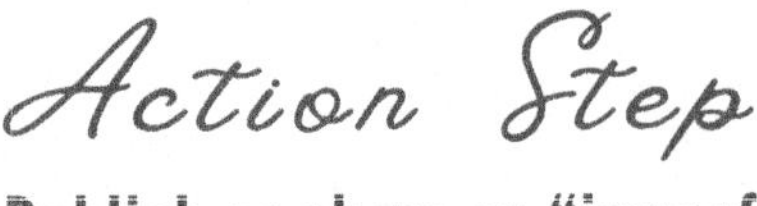

Publish or share an "imperfect" draft snippet today (100–200 words) without over-editing, choose faithfulness over perfection and move your work forward.

DAY FIFTY-ONE

God's Word Never Returns Void

Isaiah 55:11 (NLT)

"It is the same with my word. I send it out, and it always produces fruit. It will accomplish all I want it to, and it will prosper everywhere I send it."

Reflection

Every word you write for God carries weight and purpose, even when you don't see the immediate results. As writers, it's easy to wonder if your work is making any difference, especially when feedback is limited or progress feels slow. But Isaiah 55:11 is a powerful reminder that God's word, spoken or written, never returns empty. When you dedicate your writing to Him, you can trust that He will send it exactly where it needs to go and use it to accomplish His will, often in ways you may never see.

Sometimes God will use your words to encourage someone at just the right moment, or to plant a seed that grows long after you've moved on to another project. You may not always witness the fruit your writing produces, but God promises that it will prosper and fulfill its purpose. Your responsibility is to be faithful with what He gives you, allowing Him to handle the results.

Trusting God with your words means letting go of the need for instant validation and believing that He is working through you. Surrender your desire for control and recognition, and focus on obedience, writing as He leads, knowing He will multiply your efforts. Even in seasons of doubt or uncertainty, remember that nothing offered to God is ever wasted. Your faithfulness in writing for Him will bear fruit in His perfect timing.

Date:

Journal Questions

1. **When have you seen God use your words unexpectedly?**

2. **How can you trust Him with the results of your writing?**

3. **What is one area where you need to surrender the outcome of your writing to God?**

4. **Who is someone you can encourage or pray for as you trust God to use your words?**

Isaiah 55:11 (NLT)

"It is the same with my word. I send it out, and it always produces fruit. It will accomplish all I want it to, and it will prosper everywhere I send it."

Prayer

Father, in the name of Jesus,

Thank You for the privilege of writing for You. Remind me that every word I offer in obedience is used by You and never returns void. Help me trust You with the results, releasing any desire for recognition or control. Give me faith to believe that You are working through my words, even when I cannot see the outcome. Use my writing to accomplish Your will, to bear fruit in the lives of others, and to bring You glory. Strengthen my heart to surrender the results to You and to encourage others along their journey. Let my words prosper wherever You send them, and let my life be a testimony to Your faithfulness.

Amen.

Share or schedule one piece today (post, email, or excerpt) without waiting for perfect timing, and note in your journal: “I release the results to God.”

DAY FIFTY-TWO

Your Story Matters

Revelation 12:11 (NLT)

"They triumphed over him by the blood of the Lamb and by the word of their testimony..."

Reflection

Your testimony holds incredible power, far beyond what you may realize. God has woven purpose into every chapter of your life, even the parts you might prefer to keep hidden. When you share your story, your struggles, victories, and the ways God has met you in the midst of it all, you give others hope and permission to believe that healing and transformation are possible for them too.

Sometimes, fear or insecurity can make us hesitant to speak out but remember: your journey is not just for you. God can use your words to unlock freedom and encouragement in someone else's life. There is someone waiting to hear how you've overcome, how God has shown up, and how you continue to walk by faith. Don't underestimate the impact your authenticity can have on another person's path.

As you reflect on your own story, ask God for the courage to share it boldly and with humility. Trust that He will use your honesty to bring light, hope, and healing to others. Your willingness to be vulnerable is a testimony to God's faithfulness and your story truly matters in His kingdom.

Date:

Journal Questions

1. **What part of your story have you been hesitant to share?**

2. **Who might be encouraged by your testimony?**

3. **How has sharing your story in the past brought healing to you or others?**

Revelation 12:11 (NLT)

"They triumphed over him by the blood of the Lamb and by the word of their testimony..."

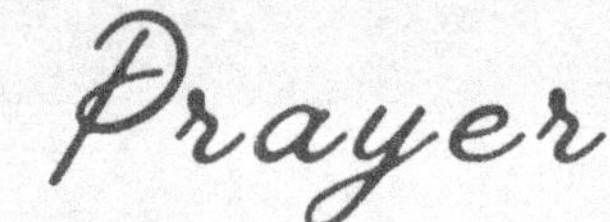

Father, in the name of Jesus,

Thank You for writing my story and redeeming every part of it. Give me the courage to share my testimony for Your glory. Help me trust that You can use even the broken places in my life to bring hope and healing to others. Let my words point people to Your goodness and faithfulness. Use my story as a light for those who need encouragement, and remind me that nothing in my journey is wasted when surrendered to You.

Amen.

Action Step

Choose one testimony moment (a struggle and how God met you) and draft a 150–200 word post or paragraph to share this week.

DAY FIFTY-THREE

The Power of Gratitude

1 Thessalonians 5:18 (NLT)

"Be thankful in all circumstances, for this is God's will for you who belong to Christ Jesus."

Reflection

Gratitude is a powerful force that can transform your entire writing journey. When you choose to thank God for every opportunity, lesson, and even the challenges, your perspective shifts from frustration to faith. Gratitude opens your heart to see God's hand at work in every detail whether you're celebrating a milestone or navigating a tough season.

Thankfulness isn't just for the easy moments; it's a discipline that sustains you through difficulties. When you practice gratitude, you invite God's peace and presence into your process.

Every blessing, every setback, and every lesson is shaping you into the writer He's called you to be. Let gratitude be the lens through which you view your journey, knowing that God is using it all for your good and His glory.

Date:

Journal Questions

1. **What are you grateful for in your writing life today?**

2. **How can you cultivate gratitude in difficult seasons?**

3. **In what ways has gratitude helped you recognize God's faithfulness in your writing journey?**

1 Thessalonians 5:18 (NLT)

"Be thankful in all circumstances, for this is God's will for you who belong to Christ Jesus."

Prayer

Father, in the name of Jesus,

Thank You for every blessing and every challenge along my writing journey. Help me see Your hand at work in all things and develop a heart of gratitude, no matter the season. Let thankfulness shape my attitude, my words, and my perspective. Use my gratitude to draw me closer to You and to encourage others through my writing.

Amen.

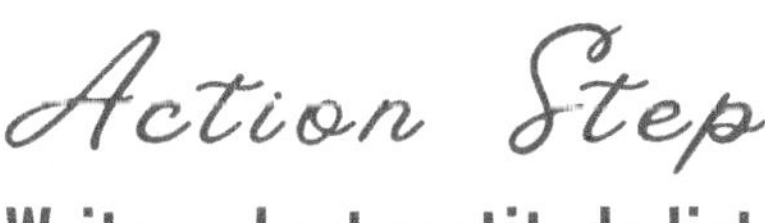

Write a short gratitude list of five items related to your writing today (wins, lessons, helpers) and place it where you draft to anchor your perspective in thankfulness.

DAY FIFTY-FOUR

Letting Go of Comparison

Galatians 6:4 (NLT)

"Pay careful attention to your own work, for then you will get the satisfaction of a job well done, and you won't need to compare yourself to anyone else."

Reflection

Comparing yourself to others is one of the quickest ways to lose your joy and confidence as a writer. God has given you a unique journey, a distinct voice, and a story that only you can tell. When you focus on what others are doing, you risk missing the beauty, growth, and purpose in your own path.

Remember, your calling is not a competition, it's a sacred assignment. Celebrate the progress you've made, the lessons you've learned, and the ways God is shaping you along the way. Embrace your individuality, knowing that your experiences, perspective, and faith are what make your writing powerful and needed.

Let God's affirmation be enough, and trust that your story matters just as it is. Release comparison, lean into your unique voice, and let your confidence be anchored in the One who called you.

Date:

Journal Questions

1. **How has comparison affected your writing?**

2. **What makes your voice and story unique?**

3. **How can you intentionally celebrate your own growth and journey, rather than measuring yourself against others?**

Galatians 6:4 (NLT)

"Pay careful attention to your own work, for then you will get the satisfaction of a job well done, and you won't need to compare yourself to anyone else."

Prayer

Father, in the name of Jesus,

Help me to celebrate my path and not compare myself to others. Remind me that You have given me a unique voice and calling. Fill my heart with gratitude for my journey and let me find joy in the story You are writing through my life.

Amen.

Action Step

Unfollow or mute one comparison trigger today and write a 3-bullet "my lane" list (voice, audience, message) to refocus on your assignment.

DAY FIFTY-FIVE

The Joy of the Lord

Nehemiah 8:10 (NLT)

"...Don't be dejected and sad, for the joy of the Lord is your strength!"

Reflection

Joy is more than a fleeting feeling, it's a spiritual strength that God provides, especially in the midst of challenges. As a writer, there will be days of frustration, fatigue, or doubt, but God's joy is available to refresh your spirit and fuel your creativity. When you write from a place of joy, your words carry life, hope, and resilience.

Let God's joy be the wellspring that sustains you through every part of the writing journey. Celebrate the small victories, savor the moments of inspiration, and invite God to fill you with His joy each day.

The more you lean into His joy, the more perseverance and creativity you'll find—even when the work feels hard. Remember, your joy in the Lord is a powerful testimony that can shine through every page you write.

Date:

Journal Questions

1. **What brings you joy in the writing process?**

2. **How can you invite more joy into your work?**

3. **In what ways can you choose joy even when writing feels difficult or discouraging?**

Nehemiah 8:10 (NLT)

"...Don't be dejected and sad, for the joy of the Lord is your strength!"

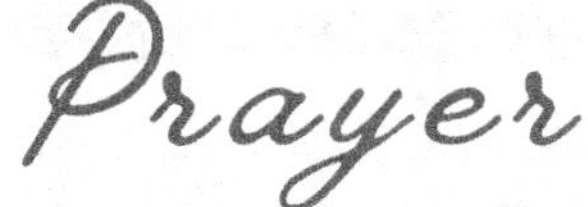

Father, in the name of Jesus,

Fill me with Your joy as I write. Let Your joy be my strength, fueling my creativity and perseverance. Help me celebrate every step of this journey and reflect Your joy in every word I share.

Amen.

Action Step

Create a "joy cue" before writing today, play one uplifting worship song or revisit a favorite passage, then write 150 words while that joy is fresh.

DAY FIFTY-SIX

The Discipline of Consistency

Proverbs 13:4 (NLT)

"Lazy people want much but get little, but those who work hard will prosper."

Reflection

Small, consistent steps lead to big results. It's easy to underestimate the power of faithfulness in the little things, but real momentum is built through steady, diligent effort. As a writer, showing up regularly, whether to jot down a paragraph, brainstorm ideas, or revise a page, creates a rhythm that carries you forward, even on days when inspiration feels distant.

Consistency isn't about perfection; it's about commitment. Every time you choose to write, even when it's hard or inconvenient, you're investing in your calling and planting seeds for future growth. Think about other areas where consistency has helped you mature, whether in faith, relationships, or work.

The same principle applies to your writing journey. Trust that God honors your faithfulness, and that over time, your small steps will add up to a harvest of creativity, impact, and fulfillment.

Date:

Journal Questions

1. **What writing habit could you commit to daily or weekly?**

2. **How has consistency helped you grow in other areas?**

3. **What obstacles tend to disrupt your writing routine, and how can you overcome them with God's help?**

Proverbs 13:4 (NLT)

"Lazy people want much but get little, but those who work hard will prosper."

Prayer

Father, in the name of Jesus,

Help me to be faithful and consistent in my writing. Give me the discipline to show up, even when motivation is low, and the perseverance to keep moving forward. Remind me that You multiply my small efforts and use them for Your glory. Let my consistency become a testimony of my commitment to the calling You've placed on my life.

Amen.

Action Step

Set a simple daily target (like 10 minutes or 150 words) and track it for the next 7 days, no skips, just show up and mark it done.

DAY FIFTY-SEVEN

The Courage to Start Again

Lamentations 3:22-23 (NLT)

"The faithful love of the Lord never ends! His mercies never cease. Great is his faithfulness; his mercies begin afresh each morning."

Reflection

God's mercies are new every morning. No matter how many times you've paused, gotten discouraged, or stopped writing altogether, you can always begin again. His compassion for you never runs out, and every day is a fresh invitation to move forward in your calling.

Don't let past setbacks or unfinished drafts keep you from embracing today's opportunities. The courage to start again is a gift of grace, one that reminds you that your story isn't over. God delights in your willingness to begin anew, trusting Him with each step.

Let His faithfulness inspire you to take that next step, no matter how small, and remember that every new beginning is a testimony of His love and mercy at work in your life. Your fresh start today is not a reset of failure, but a renewal of purpose.

Date:

Journal Questions

1. **Where do you need a fresh start in your writing?**

2. **What's one step you can take today to move forward?**

3. **How has God's faithfulness in the past given you courage to begin again now?**

Lamentations 3:22-23 (NLT)

"The faithful love of the Lord never ends! His mercies never cease. Great is his faithfulness; his mercies begin afresh each morning."

Prayer

Father, in the name of Jesus,

Thank You for new mercies and new beginnings. Give me the courage to start again, trusting in Your faithfulness and grace. Help me let go of past disappointments and move forward with hope and confidence in Your love.

Amen.

Action Step

Choose one stalled piece and add 150 new words today, no revising, just forward motion, as your tangible "begin again" moment.

DAY FIFTY-EIGHT

The Impact of a Single Word

Proverbs 25:11 (NLT)

"Timely advice is lovely, like golden apples in a silver basket."

Reflection

Never underestimate the impact of a single, Spirit-led word. Sometimes, it's the simplest message, spoken or written at just the right time, that God uses to change a life. Your words, when surrendered to the Holy Spirit, can bring encouragement, conviction, healing, or hope in ways you may never fully realize.

As a Kingdom writer, stay sensitive to God's prompting. Let Him guide your thoughts and your pen, trusting that even a brief phrase can be the answer to someone's prayer or the spark that ignites transformation.

Don't hold back what God has placed on your heart, release it in faith, knowing that your obedience can have eternal impact. Remember, your words matter, and God delights in using them for His purpose and glory. Be bold in the small moments; a short, faithful word can carry eternal weight.

Date:

Journal Questions

1. **When has a simple word or phrase impacted you deeply?**

2. **What message is God prompting you to share today?**

3. **How can you become more attentive to the Holy Spirit's leading in your daily conversations and writing?**

Proverbs 25:11 (NLT)

"Timely advice is lovely, like golden apples in a silver basket."

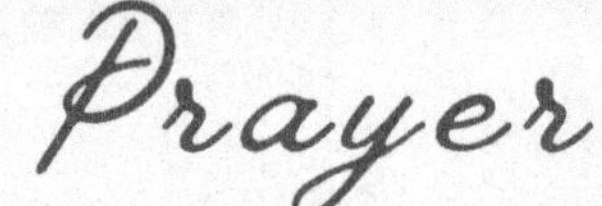

Prayer

Father, in the name of Jesus,

Holy Spirit, guide my words for Your purpose. Help me to be sensitive to Your leading and to speak or write what You place on my heart. Use my words to bring encouragement, healing, and hope to those who need it. Let every message I share be fitly spoken and bring glory to Your name.

Amen.

Action Step

Write and share one concise, Spirit-led sentence today (a text, post, or note) aimed at encouraging a specific person God brings to mind.

DAY FIFTY-NINE

The Blessing of Surrender

Romans 12:1 (NLT)

"And so, dear brothers and sisters, I plead with you to give your bodies to God because of all he has done for you. Let them be a living and holy sacrifice, the kind he will find acceptable. This is truly the way to worship him."

Reflection

Surrender is at the heart of a Kingdom writer's journey. God doesn't just want the polished parts of your writing, He wants it all: your ideas, your drafts, your fears, and even your unfinished stories. When you lay your writing on the altar, you invite God to shape, prune, and use it as He wills. Sometimes surrender means letting go of your own expectations, preferences, or timelines and trusting that God's plan is greater than anything you could create on your own.

True fruitfulness comes when you release control and allow God to lead, even if it means rewriting, pausing, or starting over. Remember, your words are safest and most powerful in His hands.

As you surrender, you'll discover new freedom, creativity, and purpose, knowing that your writing is a living sacrifice, an offering of worship and trust. Let your willingness to yield become the pathway where God breathes fresh life into your message.

Date:

Journal Questions

1. **What part of your writing are you holding back from God?**

2. **How can you surrender more fully to His plan?**

3. **What step can you take today to invite God's direction and presence into your writing process?**

Romans 12:1 (NLT)

"And so, dear brothers and sisters, I plead with you to give your bodies to God because of all he has done for you. Let them be a living and holy sacrifice, the kind he will find acceptable. This is truly the way to worship him."

Prayer

Father, in the name of Jesus,

**I surrender my words and ideas to You.
Shape, prune, and use my writing as You will.
Help me release control and trust Your purpose above my own plans. Let my writing be a living sacrifice — set apart for Your glory and guided by Your Spirit.**

Amen.

Choose one area to surrender today (timeline, chapter, or outcome). Write a single sentence naming what you're releasing, then take one aligned step (for example: revise, pause, or start fresh).

DAY SIXTY

The Freedom of Forgiveness

Ephesians 4:32 (NLT)

"Be kind to each other, tenderhearted, forgiving one another, just as God through Christ has forgiven you."

Reflection

Forgiveness is a gift God freely offers and it's one you need to give yourself, too. As a writer, it's easy to hold onto regrets about missed opportunities, harsh words, or projects left unfinished. But God's grace covers every mistake, both in your writing and your life. When you forgive yourself, you open the door to healing, creativity, and new beginnings.

Don't let shame or regret keep you from moving forward. Embrace the freedom that comes from God's forgiveness, and let that grace flow through you to others. Remember, the same compassion God extends to you is what He invites you to give away, whether to yourself, your readers, or those who have hurt you along the way.

Forgiveness brings release, restores hope, and creates space for God to do something new. As you let go, you make room for fresh vision and the courage to continue your calling with a lighter, freer heart.

Date:

Journal Questions

1. **What do you need to forgive yourself for as a writer?**

2. **How can you extend that grace to others?**

3. **In what ways has receiving God's forgiveness changed your perspective on your writing journey?**

Ephesians 4:32 (NLT)

"Be kind to each other, tenderhearted, forgiving one another, just as God through Christ has forgiven you."

Prayer

Father, in the name of Jesus,

Thank You for forgiving me completely and unconditionally. Help me forgive myself for past mistakes and walk in the freedom of Your grace. Teach me to extend that same compassion and forgiveness to others, so my heart and my writing reflect Your love.

Amen.

Action Step

Write a brief release statement to yourself about one regret (for example, "I forgive myself for..."), date it, and place it in your journal—then take one small step forward on that project today.

DAY SIXTY-ONE

The Beauty of Simplicity

Matthew 6:34 (NLT)

"So don't worry about tomorrow, for tomorrow will bring its own worries. Today's trouble is enough for today."

Reflection

Simple words often carry the deepest meaning. As writers, it's easy to fall into the trap of overcomplicating our message, thinking that more elaborate language makes a greater impact. But the truth is, clarity and simplicity open the door for more people to understand and receive what God has placed on your heart.

Jesus Himself taught profound truths in the simplest ways, inviting all to listen and be transformed. When you focus on communicating clearly, you allow your readers to connect with your message on a deeper level.

Don't be afraid to strip away the excess and let the heart of your words shine through. Trust that God can use your simple, honest words to bring encouragement, wisdom, and hope.

Date:

Journal Questions

1 **How can you simplify your writing without losing depth?**

2 **What is one simple truth you want to share today?**

3 **Where might you be tempted to overcomplicate your message, and how can you return to clarity and authenticity?**

Matthew 6:34 (NLT)

"So don't worry about tomorrow, for tomorrow will bring its own worries. Today's trouble is enough for today."

Prayer

Father, in the name of Jesus,

Help me to communicate with clarity and simplicity. Remove any pressure to impress and let my words reflect the truth and beauty of Your message. Use my writing to reach hearts and minds and let Your wisdom shine through every sentence.

Amen.

Action Step

Choose one paragraph from your current draft and simplify it, shorten sentences, remove jargon, and replace one complex idea with a clear, everyday example.

DAY SIXTY-TWO

The Value of Waiting

Psalm 27:14 (NLT)

"Wait patiently for the Lord. Be brave and courageous. Yes, wait patiently for the Lord."

Reflection

Waiting on God is never wasted time. Though it can be challenging to pause when you want to move forward, God uses seasons of waiting to prepare you and your message for greater impact. In the waiting, He refines your character, deepens your trust, and often gives you new insights that will shape your writing in powerful ways.

Instead of seeing waiting as a setback, embrace it as an opportunity for growth. Ask God what He wants to teach you in this season. Use the time to develop your skills, nurture your relationship with Him, and listen for fresh direction.

Remember, God's timing is perfect, and the message He's placed in your heart will be released at just the right moment for those who need it most. Trust the process, prepare faithfully, and let patience become part of your anointing.

Date:

Journal Questions

1. **What has God taught you in seasons of waiting?**

2. **How can you use this time to grow as a writer?**

3. **In what ways can you shift your perspective to see waiting as preparation rather than delay?**

Psalm 27:14 (NLT)

"Wait patiently for the Lord. Be brave and courageous. Yes, wait patiently for the Lord."

Prayer

Father, in the name of Jesus,

Teach me to wait on You with hope and trust. Help me embrace seasons of waiting as opportunities for growth and preparation. Strengthen my heart, deepen my faith, and prepare both me and my message for the purpose You have ahead.

Amen.

Action Step

Identify one "waiting task" (skill practice, research, or outline work) and spend 20 focused minutes on it today, treating the wait as preparation, not delay.

DAY SIXTY-THREE

The Power of Prayer

James 5:16 (NLT)

"The earnest prayer of a righteous person has great power and produces wonderful results."

Reflection

Prayer is the foundation of every Kingdom Writer's journey. Before you write a single word, covering your process in prayer invites God to lead, inspire, and anoint your work. Prayer is more than a routine, it's how you align your heart with God's will, surrender your fears, and invite His wisdom into every page.

When you pray over your writing, you're not just asking for creativity or clarity; you're inviting the Holy Spirit to breathe life into your message and to reach those who need it most. Prayer transforms your process, guards your motives, and brings peace in moments of doubt or frustration.

Remember, your writing is most powerful when it flows from a place of communion with God. Let prayer be the rhythm that steadies your heart, sharpens your focus, and fuels your words with grace and authority.

Date:

Journal Questions

1. **How has prayer shaped your writing process?**

2. **What would you like to pray over your current project?**

3. **In what ways do you sense God responding to your prayers as you write?**

James 5:16 (NLT)

"The earnest prayer of a righteous person has great power and produces wonderful results."

Prayer

Father, in the name of Jesus,

I invite You into every part of my writing. Guide my thoughts, inspire my words, and let Your Spirit lead every step of the process. Cover my project with Your wisdom and grace and use my writing to fulfill Your purpose. Let prayer always be the foundation of my journey as a Kingdom Writer.

Amen.

Action Step

Create a pre-writing prayer cue today, write a 2–3 line prayer you'll speak before each session, and tape it at your workspace to make it your consistent starting point.

DAY SIXTY-FOUR

The Gift of Rest

Psalm 23:2-3 (NLT)

"He lets me rest in green meadows; he leads me beside peaceful streams. He renews my strength. He guides me along right paths, bringing honor to his name."

Reflection

Rest is both holy and necessary. In a world that glorifies hustle and constant productivity, God gently calls you to pause, breathe, and be renewed. True rest isn't just about physical relaxation, it's about allowing God to restore your soul, refresh your creativity, and realign your perspective.

As a writer, it's easy to push through exhaustion or ignore the signs that you need a break. But neglecting rest can drain your inspiration and make your words feel empty. Embrace rest as a gift from your Shepherd, who knows exactly what you need.

When you build rhythms of rest into your life and writing routine, you make space for God to fill you anew, so you can pour out His truth and encouragement to others. Let rest become a faithful practice that protects your joy, sharpens your focus, and sustains your calling.

Date:

Journal Questions

1. **What does rest look like for you?**

2. **How can you build rest into your writing routine?**

3. **In what ways has God refreshed or restored you in past seasons when you chose to rest?**

Psalm 23:2-3 (NLT)

"He lets me rest in green meadows; he leads me beside peaceful streams. He renews my strength. He guides me along right paths, bringing honor to his name."

Prayer

Father, in the name of Jesus,

Shepherd, lead me beside still waters and restore my soul. Remind me that rest is not a weakness, but a holy invitation to receive Your renewal. Help me honor my need for rest physically, emotionally, and spiritually so I can write from a place of wholeness and peace.

Amen.

Schedule one restorative block today (20–30 minutes) step away from screens, take a walk or nap, and return to your draft only after that intentional rest.

DAY SIXTY-FIVE

The Importance of Listening

Proverbs 19:20 (NLT)

"Get all the advice and instruction you can, so you will be wise the rest of your life."

Reflection

Listening is an essential part of every writer's journey. Before you can write words that truly resonate, you must learn to listen, first to God, then to others, and also to your own heart. Listening positions you to receive wisdom, insight, and inspiration that you might otherwise miss.

When you take time to listen to God's voice, you open yourself to divine direction and fresh revelation. Listening to others helps you understand their needs, struggles, and dreams, allowing your words to meet them right where they are.

And when you listen to your own heart, you become more aware of what God is stirring within you, making your writing authentic and impactful. Remember, powerful writing is birthed from a posture of humility and attentiveness. Let listening be the foundation that precedes every word you share.

Date:

Journal Questions

1. **How can you become a better listener as a writer?**

2. **What is God speaking to you today?**

3. **In what ways can listening to others' stories or feedback enrich your writing and your ministry?**

Proverbs 19:20 (NLT)

"Get all the advice and instruction you can, so you will be wise the rest of your life."

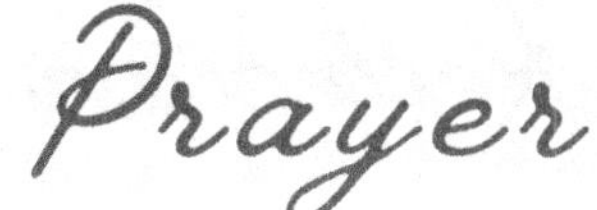

Father, in the name of Jesus,

Give me ears to hear Your voice above all else. Teach me to listen attentively—to You, to others, and to my own heart — so my writing may be guided by wisdom, compassion, and truth. Let every word I share flow from a place of deep listening and obedience to Your Spirit.

Amen.

Action Step

Schedule a 10-minute "listening triad" today, 3 minutes to sit quietly before God, 3 minutes to ask one person a thoughtful question and listen, 3 minutes to journal what's stirring in your own heart, then write one paragraph from what you heard.

DAY SIXTY-SIX

The Strength of Humility

Philippians 2:3 (NLT)

"Don't be selfish; don't try to impress others. Be humble, thinking of others as better than yourselves."

Reflection

Humility is a strength, not a weakness. As a writer, it's easy to get caught up in striving for recognition or comparing your journey to others. But humility opens doors for God's favor and positions you to receive His guidance, wisdom, and promotion in His perfect timing. When you willingly lay down pride and choose to serve others through your words, you make room for God to work in and through you.

True humility means acknowledging that your gifts, opportunities, and inspiration all come from God. It's trusting Him to lift you up and open the right doors at the right time.

Often, the most unexpected blessings flow from moments when you choose to be teachable, to listen, and to put others before yourself. Let humility shape your writing journey and keep your heart open to God's leading, He will honor your surrender and use your words for His glory.

Date:

Journal Questions

1. **Where do you need to humble yourself in your writing journey?**

2. **How has humility brought you unexpected blessings?**

3. **What is one practical way you can serve or encourage another writer this week?**

Philippians 2:3 (NLT)

"Don't be selfish; don't try to impress others. Be humble, thinking of others as better than yourselves."

Prayer

Father, in the name of Jesus,

Keep me humble and open to Your leading. Remind me that every gift and opportunity comes from You. Help me serve others with my words and trust You to lift me up in due time. Let humility be the foundation of my writing and my life, so that You alone are glorified.

Amen.

Ask one trusted peer for feedback on a current piece, receive it with a teachable spirit, and apply one suggestion today.

DAY SIXTY-SEVEN

The Blessing of Boundaries

Proverbs 4:23 (NLT)

"Guard your heart above all else, for it determines the course of your life."

Reflection

Healthy boundaries are a blessing, not a burden. They protect your time, energy, and creativity, allowing you to steward your calling as a writer with wisdom and intention. When you set boundaries, you create space for God to speak, for your ideas to flourish, and for your heart to stay refreshed and focused.

Guarding your heart and your writing space means saying "no" to distractions, unhealthy expectations, or anything that drains your passion. It also means communicating your needs clearly to others, so they can support your journey rather than unintentionally hinder it.

Remember, boundaries are not about shutting people out, they're about honoring what God has entrusted to you. When you protect your time and energy, you're able to pour out your best for the Lord and those He's called you to reach.

Date:

Journal Questions

1 **What boundaries do you need to set for your writing life?**

2 **How can you communicate those boundaries with others?**

3 **In what ways can you guard your heart from discouragement or distraction as you pursue your calling?**

Proverbs 4:23 (NLT)

"Guard your heart above all else, for it determines the course of your life."

Father, in the name of Jesus,

Help me to guard my heart and time wisely. Give me the courage to set healthy boundaries that protect my creativity and calling. Teach me to communicate my needs with grace and to honor the space You've given me for writing. Let my boundaries be a blessing to both myself and those around me, so I can serve You with excellence and joy.

Amen.

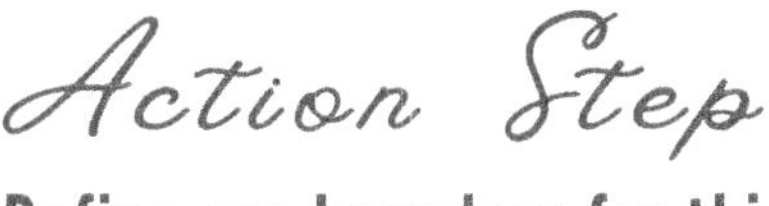

Define one boundary for this week (time block, notification limits, or a clear "office hours" message) and communicate it to the necessary people, then honor it for the next 7 days.

DAY SIXTY-EIGHT

The Hope of the Resurrection

1 Peter 1:3 (NLT)

"All praise to God, the Father of our Lord Jesus Christ. It is by his great mercy that we have been born again, because God raised Jesus Christ from the dead. Now we live with great expectation."

Reflection

The resurrection of Jesus is the foundation of our living hope. It's not just a historical event, it's the reason we can write, dream, and live with expectation and purpose. Because Christ rose, every word you write can carry the promise of new beginnings, restoration, and eternal possibility.

Let the truth of the resurrection fill your writing with life. When you share from a place of hope, you invite your readers to see beyond their present struggles and believe in God's power to redeem, restore, and renew.

Your words can be a vessel of hope, offering light to those walking through darkness. Remember, the resurrection means nothing is impossible with God, let that hope echo through every page.

Date:

Journal Questions

1. **How does the resurrection inspire your writing?**

2. **What hope can you offer your readers today?**

3. **In what ways can you allow resurrection hope to shape your perspective, even in difficult seasons?**

1 Peter 1:3 (NLT)

"All praise to God, the Father of our Lord Jesus Christ. It is by his great mercy that we have been born again, because God raised Jesus Christ from the dead. Now we live with great expectation."

Prayer

Father, in the name of Jesus,

Fill me with resurrection hope. Let the truth of Your victory over death inspire every word I write and every story I share. Help me to offer hope and possibility to my readers, reminding them that with You, all things are made new.

Amen.

Write one paragraph today that highlights a "new beginning" theme in your current project, pointing clearly to resurrection hope and restoration.

DAY SIXTY-NINE

The Influence of Encouragement

Hebrews 10:24-25 (NLT)

"Let us think of ways to motivate one another to acts of love and good works. And let us not neglect our meeting together, as some people do, but encourage one another, especially now that the day of his return is drawing near."

Reflection

Encouragement is a powerful force that can change the course of someone's day—or even their life. As a writer, your words have the ability to spur others on toward love, hope, and good deeds. God calls you to be intentional about building others up, using your writing as a tool to inspire, strengthen, and motivate.

Think back on your own journey, how a timely word of encouragement helped you keep going, or how someone's support reignited your passion. You have the same opportunity to be that spark for someone else. Let your writing reflect a heart that seeks to lift others, pointing them to God's love and reminding them they are not alone.

Every note of encouragement you write is a seed of hope that God can multiply in ways you may never fully see. Keep sowing these seeds faithfully, trusting that God will use your words to strengthen weary hearts and stir fresh courage.

Date:

Journal Questions

1. **Who can you encourage through your writing this week?**

2. **How has encouragement impacted your journey?**

3. **What practical steps can you take to make encouragement a regular part of your writing and your relationships?**

Hebrews 10:24-25 (NLT)

"Let us think of ways to motivate one another to acts of love and good works. And let us not neglect our meeting together, as some people do, but encourage one another, especially now that the day of his return is drawing near."

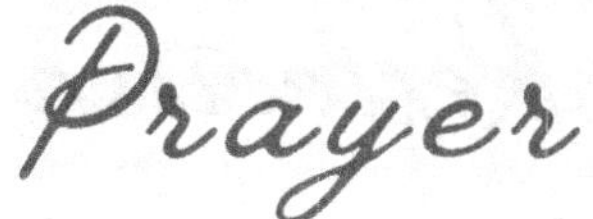

Prayer

Father, in the name of Jesus,

Make me an encourager in all I say and do. Fill my words with hope, love, and inspiration. Use my writing to spur others on toward good deeds and deeper faith. Help me recognize those who need encouragement and be faithful in building them up for Your glory.

Amen.

Action Step

Send a brief, specific encouragement to one person today (text, DM, or note), naming a strength you see in them and how it's impacting others.

DAY SEVENTY

The Gift of Generosity

2 Corinthians 9:7 (NLT)

"You must each decide in your heart how much to give. And don't give reluctantly or in response to pressure. For God loves a person who gives cheerfully."

Reflection

Generosity isn't just about money, it's a lifestyle that reflects God's heart. As a writer, you have so much more to give than finances. Your time, wisdom, encouragement, and creativity can be a blessing to others in ways you may never fully realize. When you share what you have, whether it's a listening ear, a word of advice, or a story that inspires—you multiply the impact of your gifts and spread God's love through your actions.

Ask God to show you opportunities to be generous with your words and your presence this week. Sometimes the smallest act of kindness or the simplest encouragement can make a world of difference for someone else. Remember, cheerful generosity comes from a heart that knows everything we have is a gift from God.

As you pour out, trust that He will continue to fill you, equipping you to bless others again and again. Let your generosity set the tone of your writing life, open-handed, others-focused, and rooted in love.

Date:

Journal Questions

1. **How can you be generous with your gifts this week?**

2. **Who might benefit from your encouragement or expertise?**

3. **In what ways has someone's generosity impacted your journey, and how can you pay it forward?**

2 Corinthians 9:7 (NLT)

"You must each decide in your heart how much to give. And don't give reluctantly or in response to pressure. For God loves a person who gives cheerfully."

Prayer

Father, in the name of Jesus,

Make me generous in every way. Open my eyes to opportunities to share my time, wisdom, and creativity with others. Help me to give freely and cheerfully, knowing that every act of generosity reflects Your love. Use my words and my actions to bless and encourage those around me.

Amen.

Action Step

Offer one act of creative generosity today (share a tip, give feedback, gift a resource, or send an encouraging note) to a writer or reader who could use it.

DAY SEVENTY-ONE

The Power of Identity

Ephesians 2:10 (NLT)

"For we are God's masterpiece. He has created us anew in Christ Jesus, so we can do the good things he planned for us long ago."

Reflection

You are God's workmanship, a masterpiece, uniquely designed and crafted for a divine purpose. Your value and identity are not determined by your accomplishments, failures, or the opinions of others, but by who you are in Christ. When you write from this place of true identity, your words carry authenticity, authority, and impact.

Embracing your identity in Christ means letting go of old labels, insecurities, and self-doubt. It's about believing that God has equipped you with everything you need to fulfill your calling as a writer. When you understand who you are in Him, you can write with confidence, creativity, and freedom, knowing your voice matters and your story has purpose.

Let your writing reflect the truth of your identity, and trust that God will use your words to accomplish the good works He's prepared just for you. Stand firm in who you are, and let your God-given identity shape every sentence you write.

Date:

Journal Questions

1. **What truths about your identity do you need to embrace?**

2. **How can you write from a place of confidence in Christ?**

3. **In what areas do you struggle to believe you are God's workmanship, and how can you invite Him to renew your perspective?**

Ephesians 2:10 (NLT)

"For we are God's masterpiece. He has created us anew in Christ Jesus, so we can do the good things he planned for us long ago."

Prayer

Father, in the name of Jesus,

Remind me who I am in You. Help me embrace my true identity as Your workmanship, created for a purpose. Let my writing flow from a place of confidence in Christ, and use my words to fulfill the good works You have prepared for me.

Amen.

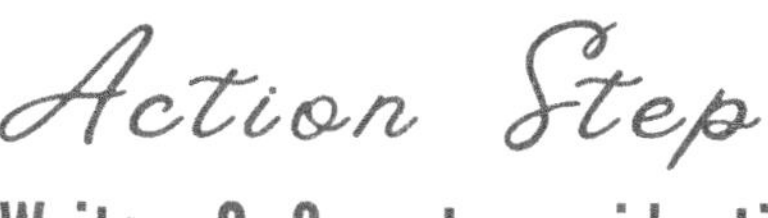

Write a 2–3 sentence identity declaration (for example, "In Christ, I am His workmanship with a needed voice"), place it at the top of today's draft, and write 150 words from that posture.

DAY SEVENTY-TWO

The Blessing of Contentment

Philippians 4:11 (NLT)

"Not that I was ever in need, for I have learned how to be content with whatever I have."

Reflection

Contentment is a rare and beautiful blessing, especially in a world obsessed with numbers, recognition, and constant striving. As a Kingdom writer, true peace comes not from applause or achievement, but from resting in God's approval and purpose for your life. When you let go of comparison and the pressure to measure your worth by external standards, you make room for God's perfect peace to guard your heart.

Contentment doesn't mean settling or losing ambition, it means trusting that God's timing, provision, and affirmation are enough. It's choosing gratitude for what you have and where you are, believing that every season has value.

As you write, let your heart be anchored in thankfulness and quiet trust, knowing that God sees your faithfulness and delights in your obedience, no matter the size of your audience. Let contentment steady your pace and purify your motives as you serve with your words.

Date:

Journal Questions

1. **Where do you struggle with contentment in your writing?**

2. **How can you cultivate a grateful heart?**

3. **What practical steps can you take to focus on God's approval rather than chasing recognition or numbers?**

Philippians 4:11 (NLT)

"Not that I was ever in need, for I have learned how to be content with whatever I have."

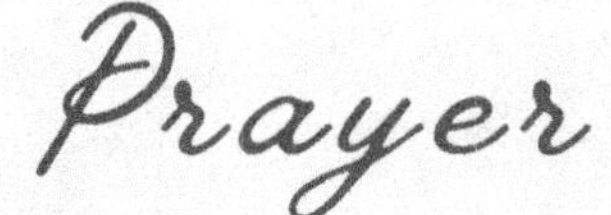

Father, in the name of Jesus,

Teach me to be content in every season. Help me rest in Your approval and trust Your timing and provision. Fill my heart with gratitude and peace, and let my writing be an offering of thankfulness for all You have done.

Amen.

Action Step

Do a contentment reset: list three things you're grateful for in this season of writing, close your metrics tab for the day, and complete one focused session from that posture.

DAY SEVENTY-THREE

The Miracle of Small Beginnings

Zechariah 4:10 (NLT)

"Do not despise these small beginnings, for the Lord rejoices to see the work begin..."

Reflection

Don't despise small beginnings. Every big dream or finished book starts with a single step, a first word, a new idea, a tentative outline. God delights in your willingness to begin, even when it feels insignificant or slow. The miracle is not just in the finished product, but in the faithful steps you take along the way.

It's easy to overlook or minimize early progress, especially when results seem far off. But remember, God sees and celebrates every act of obedience, every page written, and every seed sown.

Nurture what He's given you, no matter how small it seems. Celebrate your progress, trust that God is multiplying your efforts and know that beginnings are sacred ground for miracles.

Date:

Journal Questions

1 **What "small" thing are you starting or nurturing right now?**

2 **How can you celebrate progress, not just results?**

3 **Where have you seen God's faithfulness in turning your small beginnings into something greater?**

Zechariah 4:10 (NLT)

"Do not despise these small beginnings, for the Lord rejoices to see the work begin..."

Prayer

Father, in the name of Jesus,

Thank You for every beginning. Give me faith to honor the small steps and to trust that You delight in my progress. Help me celebrate what You are building in and through me and believe that even my smallest efforts matter in Your hands.

Amen.

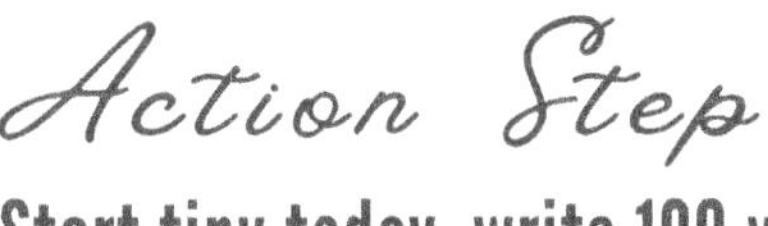

Start tiny today, write 100 words or outline three bullets and mark it as a win to honor your small beginning.

DAY SEVENTY-FOUR

The Power of Declaring Truth

Psalm 107:2 (NLT)

"Has the Lord redeemed you? Then speak out! Tell others he has redeemed you from your enemies."

Reflection

There is power in declaring God's truth, not just over your writing, but over your entire life and future. When you speak what God says about you, your calling, and your purpose, you align your heart with His promises and silence the lies of the enemy. Your words carry weight in the spiritual realm. As you boldly declare God's truth, you reinforce your identity, fuel your faith, and invite God's power to work through your writing.

Don't be afraid to speak life over your journey, even when circumstances seem to contradict what God has promised. Let your declarations shape your mindset, your creativity, and the impact of your words.

Remember, as the redeemed of the Lord, your story is a testimony to God's faithfulness, declare it with confidence and watch how He moves. Let your spoken truth set the tone for your process and the atmosphere of your writing space.

Date:

Journal Questions

1. **What truth do you need to declare today?**

2. **How can you speak life over your writing?**

3. **In what areas have you allowed doubt or negativity to take root, and how can you replace those with declarations of God's promises?**

Psalm 107:2 (NLT)

"Has the Lord redeemed you? Then speak out! Tell others he has redeemed you from your enemies."

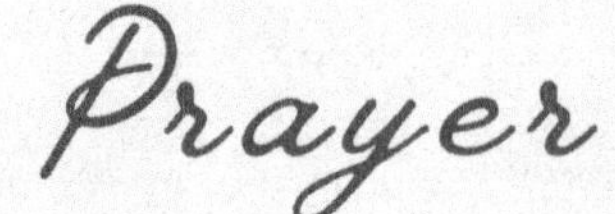

Father, in the name of Jesus,

Let my words align with Your truth. Give me the courage to declare Your promises over my life, my writing, and my future. Silence every lie of the enemy and let my declarations be a testimony of Your faithfulness and power. Use my words to bring life, hope, and transformation, to myself and to everyone who reads them.

Amen.

Write and speak a 3-line declaration over your writing (identity, assignment, outcome). Post it at your workspace and say it before today's session.

DAY SEVENTY-FIVE

The Gift of Curiosity

Proverbs 2:3-5 (NLT)

"Yes, if you call out for insight and cry aloud for understanding, and if you look for it as for silver and search for it as for hidden treasure, then you will understand what it means to fear the Lord, and you will gain knowledge of God."

Reflection

Curiosity is a gift from God that leads to discovery, growth, and deeper faith. When you nurture a curious spirit, you open yourself to new wisdom, fresh inspiration, and creative breakthroughs. Don't be afraid to ask questions, explore new perspectives, or dig deeper into topics that stir your heart.

Let your curiosity fuel your writing journey. The more you seek understanding, about your craft, your faith, or the world around you, the richer your words will become. God delights in a heart that longs to learn and grow, and He promises to reveal wisdom to those who earnestly seek it.

Stay teachable, remain open to new ideas, and trust that your curiosity will lead you closer to God's truth and purpose for your life and writing. Let exploration become part of your process, widening your perspective and sharpening your message.

Date:

Journal Questions

1. **What are you curious about in your writing or faith?**

2. **How can you pursue answers or new ideas this week?**

3. **In what ways has curiosity led you to unexpected growth or deeper understanding in the past?**

Proverbs 2:3-5 (NLT)

"Yes, if you call out for insight and cry aloud for understanding, and if you look for it as for silver and search for it as for hidden treasure, then you will understand what it means to fear the Lord, and you will gain knowledge of God."

Prayer

Father, in the name of Jesus,

Give me a curious and teachable heart. Help me ask questions, seek wisdom, and remain open to the new things You want to show me. Let my curiosity fuel my writing and draw me closer to Your truth. Guide my steps as I pursue understanding and use my discoveries to bless others through my words.

Amen.

Action Step

Choose one question that's been tugging at you and spend 15 minutes researching or interviewing someone about it, then write a 100-word insight from what you learned.

DAY SEVENTY-SIX

The Gift of Peace

John 14:27 (NLT)

"I am leaving you with a gift—peace of mind and heart. And the peace I give is a gift the world cannot give. So don't be troubled or afraid."

Reflection

God's peace is a priceless gift, available to you regardless of the chaos or uncertainty swirling around you. As a writer, it's easy to let deadlines, doubts, or distractions steal your sense of calm. But Jesus offers a peace that isn't dependent on circumstances, a peace that guards your heart and mind, keeping you steady and secure.

Let His peace be the anchor for your writing journey. When anxiety or discouragement tries to creep in, pause and invite God's presence to settle your spirit. Remind yourself that you are not alone, His Spirit is with you, guiding, comforting, and empowering you every step of the way.

Trust that His peace will protect your creativity, your focus, and your joy, enabling you to write from a place of rest and confidence. Let calm become your creative baseline, so your words flow from a steady, grounded heart.

Date:

Journal Questions

1. **What robs your peace in your writing journey?**

2. **How can you invite God's peace into your process?**

3. **What practical steps can you take to pause and receive God's peace when stress or anxiety arise?**

John 14:27 (NLT)

"I am leaving you with a gift—peace of mind and heart. And the peace I give is a gift the world cannot give. So don't be troubled or afraid."

Prayer

Father, in the name of Jesus,

Fill me with Your perfect peace. Guard my heart and mind from worry, fear, and distraction. Let Your peace be the foundation of my writing journey and help me trust You in every circumstance. May Your presence calm my spirit and empower me to write with clarity, purpose, and joy.

Amen.

Action Step

Set a "peace pause" timer for 3 minutes before writing, breathe slowly, release today's worries, and begin your session only after your heart rate and focus feel settled.

DAY SEVENTY-SEVEN

The Strength of Perseverance

James 1:12 (NLT)

"God blesses those who patiently endure testing and temptation. Afterward they will receive the crown of life that God has promised to those who love him."

Reflection

Perseverance brings reward. Every writer faces moments when motivation fades and the journey feels uphill. But it's in those very moments that your faith and commitment are strengthened. God promises a blessing for those who keep going, even when it's hard. Your perseverance is a testimony, not just to others, but to yourself, of God's sustaining power and your trust in His promises.

Remember, you are not alone. God is with you in every challenge, and He often sends others to encourage and support you along the way. Lean into His strength, celebrate every small victory, and keep your eyes on the purpose behind your writing.

The fruit of perseverance is not only in the finished work but in the growth and character built along the way. Let steady, faithful steps become your rhythm, trusting that God is shaping both your message and your maturity through the process.

Date:

Journal Questions

1 **What helps you persevere when writing feels tough?**

2 **Who can cheer you on in your journey?**

3 **How has God shown Himself faithful to you in past seasons of perseverance?**

James 1:12 (NLT)

"God blesses those who patiently endure testing and temptation. Afterward they will receive the crown of life that God has promised to those who love him."

Prayer

Father, in the name of Jesus,

Give me strength to persevere, especially when the journey feels long or difficult. Remind me of Your promises and the reward that comes from trusting You. Surround me with encouragement and help me to keep moving forward, knowing that You are with me every step of the way.

Amen.

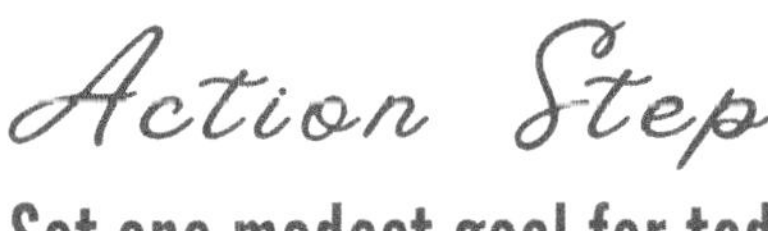

Set one modest goal for today (for example, 200 words or one edit pass), complete it, and log it in a simple streak tracker to reinforce your perseverance.

DAY SEVENTY-EIGHT

The Gift of Perspective

Colossians 3:2 (NLT)

"Think about the things of heaven, not the things of earth."

Reflection

Perspective is a powerful gift. When you set your mind on things above, you see your writing, your challenges, and your opportunities through God's eyes, not just your own. His perspective brings clarity, hope, and purpose to every season. Instead of getting caught up in disappointments or distractions, you can rest in the assurance that God's plans are bigger and better than anything you could imagine.

Shifting your focus to God's bigger picture helps you rise above discouragement and see the eternal value in your work. It reminds you that your writing is part of a greater story, one that God is weaving for His glory.

Ask Him daily to give you fresh vision, to renew your mind, and to help you see every situation from His vantage point. When you embrace God's perspective, everything changes. Let His view steady your heart and guide your next faithful step.

Date:

Journal Questions

1. **How can you shift your focus to God's bigger picture?**

2. **What new perspective do you need today?**

3. **In what area of your writing or life do you sense God inviting you to see things through His eyes?**

Colossians 3:2 (NLT)

"Think about the things of heaven, not the things of earth."

Prayer

Father, in the name of Jesus,

Give me Your perspective in all I do. Lift my thoughts above my circumstances and help me see my writing, my challenges, and my opportunities through Your eyes. Renew my mind and fill me with vision for the greater story You are writing.

Amen.

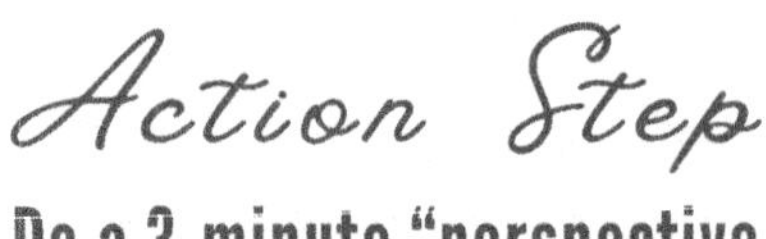

Action Step

Do a 3-minute "perspective reset" before writing, list one challenge, then write how it looks from God's bigger picture, and draft your next sentence from that vantage point.

DAY SEVENTY-NINE

The Power of Blessing

Numbers 6:24-26 (NLT)

"May the Lord bless you and protect you. May the Lord smile on you and be gracious to you. May the Lord show you his favor and give you his peace."

Reflection

There is incredible power in speaking blessings, over yourself, your writing, and your readers. When you declare God's favor, peace, and presence, you invite His supernatural work into every aspect of your journey. Blessing is more than a kind wish; it's a spiritual act that aligns your heart and your words with God's promises.

Take time today to receive God's blessing for yourself. Let His love and grace wash over you, restoring your confidence and joy. Then, extend that blessing outward, over your writing process, your creative ideas, and especially over those who will read your words.

Your blessing can become a channel of encouragement, hope, and transformation for others. Never underestimate how God can use a simple word of blessing to change a life. Let blessing shape the atmosphere of your work and the hearts of those who encounter it.

Date:

Journal Questions

1. **What blessing do you need to receive today?**

2. **Who can you bless with your words?**

3. **How can you make blessing others a regular part of your writing and your daily life?**

Numbers 6:24-26 (NLT)

"May the Lord bless you and protect you. May the Lord smile on you and be gracious to you. May the Lord show you his favor and give you his peace."

Prayer

Father, in the name of Jesus,

Let Your blessing rest on all I write. Fill me with Your peace, favor, and grace. Help me receive Your blessing for myself and speak it over my readers and everyone I encounter. Use my words to be a source of encouragement and hope and let Your presence shine through everything I create.

Amen.

Speak a 3-part blessing aloud today, over yourself, your writing session, and your readers, then write 150 words with that blessed posture.

DAY EIGHTY

The Promise of Fruitfulness

John 15:5 (NLT)

"Yes, I am the vine; you are the branches. Those who remain in me, and I in them, will produce much fruit. For apart from me you can do nothing."

Reflection

Abiding in Christ is the key to a fruitful writing journey. When you stay connected to Jesus, through prayer, worship, and dependence on His Spirit, your words will carry life, power, and lasting impact. Fruitfulness isn't measured by numbers or recognition, but by the transformation, encouragement, and hope your writing brings to others.

Don't strive to produce results in your own strength. Instead, rest in the truth that true growth and impact come from remaining close to Jesus. Let Him guide your ideas, shape your message, and multiply the reach of your words.

As you abide in Him, trust that your writing will bear fruit in ways you may never fully see—fruit that brings glory to God and blessing to His kingdom. Let connection, not performance, be the measure of your process each day.

Date:

Journal Questions

1. **How can you stay connected to Jesus as you write?**

2. **What fruit do you hope to see from your writing?**

3. **In what ways can you surrender your expectations and trust God for the results?**

John 15:5 (NLT)

"Yes, I am the vine; you are the branches. Those who remain in me, and I in them, will produce much fruit. For apart from me you can do nothing."

Prayer

Father, in the name of Jesus,

Let my work bear lasting fruit for Your kingdom. Help me to stay closely connected to You as I write. Guide my words, inspire my heart, and use my writing to bring transformation, hope, and encouragement to others. May everything I create be rooted in You and bring glory to Your name.

Amen.

Choose one abiding practice before you write today (worship song, Scripture meditation, or 5 minutes of stillness), then draft 150 words flowing from that connection.

DAY EIGHTY-ONE

The Strength of Surrender

Matthew 16:24 (NLT)

"Then Jesus said to his disciples, 'If any of you wants to be my follower, you must give up your own way, take up your cross, and follow me.'"

Reflection

Surrender is not a sign of weakness, it's the path to true strength in Christ. When you let go of control, expectations, or the desire to do things your own way, you make space for God's power to work in and through you. In your writing life, surrender means trusting God with your ideas, your process, your timeline, and your outcomes.

True freedom and strength come when you release your fears, doubts, and ambitions into God's hands. Surrender allows you to write with greater authenticity and peace, knowing that your words are guided by the One who knows the full story.

Let Christ's example of surrender inspire you to lay everything at His feet, believing that He will use your obedience for His glory. Write from a yielded heart, confident that what you release to Him, He will refine and multiply.

Date:

Journal Questions

1. **What do you need to surrender in your writing life?**

2. **How can surrender lead to greater freedom?**

3. **In what area do you sense God inviting you to trust Him more deeply through surrender?**

Matthew 16:24 (NLT)

"Then Jesus said to his disciples, 'If any of you wants to be my follower, you must give up your own way, take up your cross, and follow me.'"

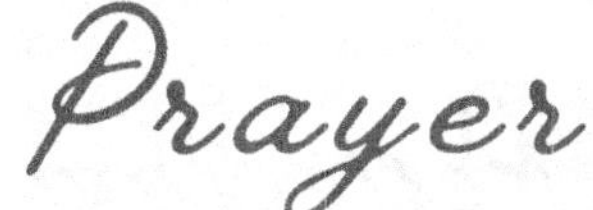

Father, in the name of Jesus,

I surrender all to You. Help me let go of my own ways and trust Your perfect plan for my writing and my life. Teach me to find true strength in surrender, and let my obedience bring You glory. Use my words as an offering, and lead me in freedom and peace.

Amen.

Action Step

Identify one area you're trying to control (timeline, feedback, or results). Name it, release it, and take one aligned step today (for example, write 150 words without checking metrics).

DAY EIGHTY-TWO

The Power of Hope

Romans 15:13 (NLT)

"I pray that God, the source of hope, will fill you completely with joy and peace because you trust in him. Then you will overflow with confident hope through the power of the Holy Spirit."

Reflection

Hope anchors your soul, especially on the days when writing feels hard or the vision seems distant. As a Kingdom writer, you are called to let God fill you with a hope that goes beyond circumstances, a hope rooted in His promises and faithfulness. When you write from a place of hope, your words become a beacon for others who need encouragement and light.

If you find yourself weary or discouraged, invite God to restore your hope. Trust that He is working in and through you, even when progress feels slow.

As you allow His hope to fill your heart, you'll find new joy, peace, and inspiration to keep going. And as a messenger of hope, your writing can point others to the God who never fails and always brings new beginnings. Let hope set the tone of your process and the message of your words.

Date:

Journal Questions

1. **Where do you need hope restored in your writing?**

2. **How can you become a messenger of hope?**

3. **What promise from God can you hold onto today to anchor your hope and inspire your words?**

Romans 15:13 (NLT)

"I pray that God, the source of hope, will fill you completely with joy and peace because you trust in him. Then you will overflow with confident hope through the power of the Holy Spirit."

Prayer

Father, in the name of Jesus,

God of hope, fill me with joy and peace as I trust in You. Restore hope in every area of my writing and help me to overflow with hope by the power of Your Spirit. Use my words to encourage others and to point them to the hope that is found in You alone.

Amen.

Action Step

Write a "hope paragraph" today that names one promise you're standing on and weaves it into your current piece, aiming to lift a weary reader.

DAY EIGHTY-THREE

The Blessing of Reflection

Psalm 77:11-12 (NLT)

"But then I recall all you have done, O Lord; I remember your wonderful deeds of long ago. They are constantly in my thoughts. I cannot stop thinking about your mighty works."

Reflection

Taking time to reflect on God's faithfulness is a powerful spiritual discipline. When you pause to remember what God has done in your writing journey, every open door, answered prayer, and moment of inspiration, you cultivate a heart of gratitude and strengthen your vision for the future. Reflection shifts your focus from what's lacking to the abundance of God's goodness and provision.

Looking back on past victories fuels hope for what's ahead. It reminds you that the same God who brought you through before will guide you again.

Let your reflections become reminders of His love, power, and unwavering presence. As you recount God's faithfulness, your gratitude will grow and your vision will be renewed for the next steps in your calling.

Date:

Journal Questions

1. **What has God done for you in your writing journey?**

2. **How can remembering past victories inspire you today?**

3. **In what ways can you make reflection a regular practice to fuel gratitude and vision?**

Psalm 77:11-12 (NLT)

"But then I recall all you have done, O Lord; I remember your wonderful deeds of long ago. They are constantly in my thoughts. I cannot stop thinking about your mighty works."

Prayer

Father, in the name of Jesus,

Thank You for Your faithfulness. Help me remember and celebrate all You have done in my life and writing. Let my reflections fill me with gratitude and inspire fresh vision for the future. Remind me daily that Your goodness endures forever.

Amen.

Create a "faithfulness log" with three specific memories of God's provision in your writing; date them, place the list in your workspace, and review it before your next session.

DAY EIGHTY-FOUR

The Call to Action

James 2:17 (NLT)

"So you see, faith by itself isn't enough. Unless it produces good deeds, it is dead and useless."

Reflection

Faith is more than belief, it's a call to action. As a Kingdom writer, it's not enough to simply dream, plan, or feel inspired. God calls you to put your faith into motion by taking practical steps forward in your writing journey. Whether it's starting a new project, sharing your work, or reaching out for support, action is what brings your vision to life.

Don't let fear or procrastination keep you from moving forward. Even small steps of obedience are powerful when they're taken in faith. Trust that as you act on what God has shown you, He will meet you with grace, provision, and new opportunities.

Let your writing journey be marked by a willingness to respond to God's promptings, moving from inspiration to implementation and watching Him work through your obedience. Keep your feet moving while your heart stays anchored in trust.

Date:

Journal Questions

1. **What action is God prompting you to take today?**

2. **How can you move from inspiration to implementation?**

3. **What small, practical step can you take this week to advance your writing journey in faith?**

James 2:17 (NLT)

"So you see, faith by itself isn't enough. Unless it produces good deeds, it is dead and useless."

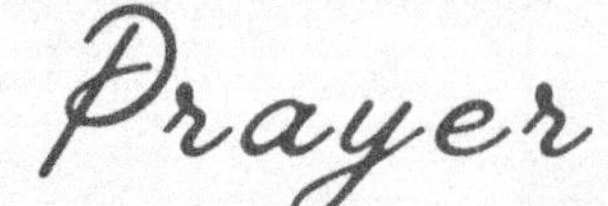

Father, in the name of Jesus,

Help me to act on what You've shown me. Give me courage to take the next step in my writing journey, trusting that You will guide and provide. Let my faith be alive and active and use my obedience to accomplish Your purpose through my words.

Amen.

Action Step

Write a 3-item "faith-in-motion" list (start, share, or ask), then complete one item today, log it as your obedience step.

DAY EIGHTY-FIVE

The Journey Continues

Philippians 1:6 (NLT)

"And I am certain that God, who began the good work within you, will continue his work until it is finally finished on the day when Christ Jesus returns."

Reflection

Your journey as a Kingdom Writer is ongoing, God's work in you is never truly finished. Every lesson, every page, and every season has been a step in His greater plan for your life and calling. Even as you reach the end of these 90 days, trust that God is still writing your story, shaping your voice, and preparing new opportunities for you to grow and serve.

Celebrate all that God has taught you on this journey. Reflect on the breakthroughs, the challenges, and the ways He's revealed Himself through your writing.

Remember, the same God who brought you this far will continue to lead, strengthen, and complete the good work He's started in you. Stay open, stay faithful, and keep saying "yes" to the next step He places before you. The best is yet to come.

Date:

Journal Questions

1. **What has God taught you through these 90 days?**

2. **What's your next step as a writer?**

3. **How can you remain open to God's ongoing work in your writing and your life?**

Philippians 1:6 (NLT)

"And I am certain that God, who began the good work within you, will continue his work until it is finally finished on the day when Christ Jesus returns."

Prayer

Father, in the name of Jesus,

Thank You for leading me through this journey. Continue Your good work in and through me. Give me faith to trust Your process and courage to take the next step. Let my writing always reflect Your love, purpose, and glory.

Amen.

Action Step

Write a brief "next 30 days" plan with three faith-filled actions (create, share, connect), and commit to the first one today.

DAY EIGHTY-SIX

Renewing Your Mind as a Writer

Romans 12:2 (NLT)

"Don't copy the behavior and customs of this world, but let God transform you into a new person by changing the way you think."

Reflection

Sometimes, the biggest battle as a writer is in your thoughts, comparison, doubt, or old narratives that hold you back. God invites you to renew your mind and let His truth shape your creativity.

Release negative patterns and invite God to fill your mind with His promises. As your thoughts are transformed, your words will reflect greater freedom, clarity, and purpose. Let God's truth be the filter for every idea and every draft.

Date:

Journal Questions

1. **What negative thought patterns do you need to surrender to God?**

2. **How can you invite God's truth to reshape your mindset as a writer?**

3. **In what ways has renewing your mind led to greater creativity or confidence?**

Romans 12:2 (NLT)

"Don't copy the behavior and customs of this world, but let God transform you into a new person by changing the way you think."

Prayer

Father, in the name of Jesus,

Renew my mind and fill my thoughts with Your truth. Help me to let go of comparison, doubt, and old stories that hold me back. Transform my thinking so that my writing flows from a place of freedom and faith. Let Your Word be the foundation of my creativity.

Amen.

Action Step

Identify one negative thought pattern that has affected your writing. Replace it with a truth from God's Word and write it at the top of your next draft.

DAY EIGHTY-SEVEN

Your Story, Someone's Comfort

2 Corinthians 1:4 (NLT)

"He comforts us in all our troubles so that we can comfort others. When they are troubled, we will be able to give them the same comfort God has given us."

Reflection

Your testimony is not just for you, it's a gift meant to bring comfort and hope to others. When you share how God has met you in your struggles, you open the door for someone else to experience healing and encouragement.

Don't underestimate the impact of your words. Even a simple story of God's faithfulness can be the encouragement someone else needs to keep going. Be bold in sharing, trusting that God will use your honesty to bring light and comfort to those who are hurting.

Date:

Journal Questions

1. **Who in your life could benefit from hearing your story?**

2. **How has God used someone else's testimony to comfort you?**

3. **What fears do you need to surrender in order to share your story more freely?**

2 Corinthians 1:4 (NLT)

"He comforts us in all our troubles so that we can comfort others. When they are troubled, we will be able to give them the same comfort God has given us."

Prayer

Father, in the name of Jesus,

Thank You for comforting me in every season. Give me the courage to share my story so that others may find hope. Use my testimony as a channel of Your love and encouragement. Help me to trust You with the impact and to remember that my story matters in Your kingdom.

Amen.

Action Step

Write a short note or post sharing a lesson from your journey, with the intention of encouraging someone who may need it today.

DAY EIGHTY-EIGHT

The Courage to Risk for God

Joshua 1:9 (NLT)

"This is my command, be strong and courageous! Do not be afraid or discouraged. For the Lord your God is with you wherever you go."

Reflection

Sometimes, sacrifice means stepping out of your comfort zone, writing the hard story, sharing your work publicly, or following God into new creative territory. God honors your willingness to obey, even when it feels risky. Each act of courage is an offering that invites His presence and power into your journey.

Don't let fear of the unknown or desire for safety hold you back from what God is calling you to do. Trust that He is with you, equipping you for every step. Your creative risks become seeds for future growth, breakthroughs, and blessings.

Date:

Journal Questions

1. **What creative risk have you been hesitant to take in your writing?**

2. **How might obedience in this area open new doors for growth?**

3. **What does it look like to trust God with the outcome, even if it feels uncertain?**

Joshua 1:9 (NLT)

"This is my command, be strong and courageous! Do not be afraid or discouraged. For the Lord your God is with you wherever you go."

Prayer

Father, in the name of Jesus,

Thank You for calling me to boldness and faith. Give me the courage to take creative risks for Your glory. Help me to trust You with the outcome and to step forward even when I feel afraid. Use my obedience to open new doors and to accomplish Your purpose through my writing.

Amen.

Action Step

Identify one creative risk you've been avoiding. Take a small, courageous step toward it today, trusting God's presence as you move forward.

DAY EIGHTY-NINE

Writing as Worship

Colossians 3:23 (NLT)

"Work willingly at whatever you do, as though you were working for the Lord rather than for people."

Reflection

Writing can be an act of worship when you offer it wholeheartedly to God. It's not just about the words you put on the page, but the spirit in which you write. When you dedicate your craft to the Lord, your writing becomes a way to honor Him and reflect His love and truth to the world.

Approaching writing as worship shifts your perspective from performance to presence. It's less about striving for perfection and more about inviting God into the process. Whether you're working on a book, a blog, or a simple journal entry, let your heart's posture be one of gratitude and devotion.

Ask God to fill your words with His Spirit and to use your writing to draw others closer to Him. When you write as an act of worship, you'll find deeper joy and purpose in every project.

Date:

Journal Questions

1. How can you intentionally turn your writing time into an act of worship?

2. In what ways has writing drawn you closer to God?

3. What distractions or pressures do you need to release in order to write for God's glory?

Colossians 3:23 (NLT)

"Work willingly at whatever you do, as though you were working for the Lord rather than for people."

Father, in the name of Jesus,

Thank You for the gift of writing. Help me approach every project as an act of worship to You. Fill my words with Your Spirit and let my writing bring You honor. Free me from distractions and pressures and let my heart be focused on pleasing You above all else.

Amen.

Action Step

Create a brief "worship preface" for today's session, write 2–3 lines dedicating your work to God, then begin your draft from that posture.

DAY NINETY

Stepping Into the New

Isaiah 43:19 (NLT)

"For I am about to do something new. See, I have already begun! Do you not see it?"

Reflection

The journey doesn't end here; God has new things ahead for you as a writer. Each day is an invitation to step into the "new" He is preparing. Daily surrender is now your foundation, giving you the freedom to embrace new opportunities, ideas, and adventures in faith.

Trust that God is already at work, making a way for you. Let go of old patterns, fears, or routines that no longer serve you, and make room for His creative work in your life. The best is yet to come when you walk forward in His newness.

Date:

Journal Questions

1. **What "new thing" is God stirring in your heart for your writing journey?**

2. **How can you prepare your mind and heart to embrace change?**

3. **In what ways will you continue the habit of daily surrender as you step forward?**

Isaiah 43:19 (NLT)

"For I am about to do something new. See, I have already begun! Do you not see it?"

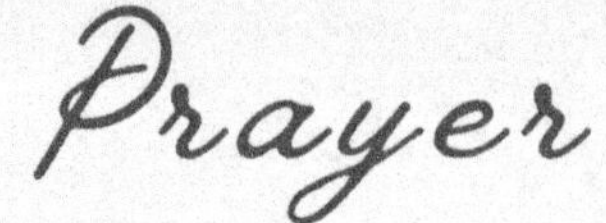

Father, in the name of Jesus,

Thank You for the promise of new beginnings. Help me to let go of the old and to welcome the new things You are doing in my life and writing. Give me faith to step forward with confidence, trusting Your guidance every day. May my journey continue to be marked by surrender, courage, and hope.

Amen.

Action Step

Write a sentence about the "new thing" you sense God calling you to next. Dedicate your next writing session to this fresh direction and invite God to lead you into it.

Date:

Date:

Date:

Date:

Date:

Date:

Date:

Date:

Date:

Date:

Closing Reflections

Your Greatest Decision

As you reach the end of this Transformative Reflection Journal, I invite you to pause, breathe, and consider one of the most meaningful decisions you'll ever face, not just as a writer, but as a person seeking purpose, healing, and transformation.

This final section isn't just a conclusion; it's an invitation. Whether you've been reflecting on your faith for years or are just beginning to explore what a relationship with God could look like, this is your space to consider a new step forward. My hope is that you read these words not as a ritual, but as a genuine opportunity for change, growth, and true connection.

The Gifts That Await

Before you move on, take a moment to reflect on the remarkable gifts that God offers to anyone who opens their heart to Him. These are not abstract ideas, they are real, practical mercies that can shape your writing, your relationships, and your daily life.

- **Knowledge**: God's Word is a guiding light. The Bible isn't just a book; it's a source of wisdom and clarity for the journey ahead (Romans 1:16-17).
- **Time & Patience**: God gives us space to grow. His kindness gives us time to learn, change, and return to Him again and again (Romans 2:3-4).
- **Redemption**: Jesus' sacrifice frees us from the weight of our mistakes. Through Him, we are offered a fresh start (Romans 3:24).
- **Remission**: We are set free from the penalties of our past. God's forgiveness is complete and unconditional (Romans 3:25).
- **Justification**: The moment you accept Christ, you are seen as righteous, your identity is forever changed (Romans 3:24).
- **Freedom**: You are no longer bound by your past or by fear. Through Christ, you can live in newness and purpose (Romans 6:4).
- **No Condemnation**: There is no shame or condemnation for those who belong to Christ. The Holy Spirit is with you, guiding and strengthening you every step of the way (Romans 8:1, 8:11-13).

Workbook Reflection: Making It Personal

Take time to reflect on these gifts. How do they speak to your journey as a writer? How do they connect to the stories you want to tell, the healing you seek, or the purpose you're discovering?

Use the space below to journal your thoughts, prayers, or questions. This is your moment to be honest, with yourself and with God.

Reflection Prompt:

- Which of God's gifts do you feel most drawn to right now?
- Where do you feel you need God's patience, freedom, or guidance in your writing journey?
- What would it look like to invite God into your creative process, your dreams, and your struggles?

An Invitation to Relationship

No matter where you are on your journey, you are welcome here. Maybe you've never taken the first step to know God, or perhaps you feel a gentle tug to return and reconnect after some time away. This is a safe, grace-filled space for you to explore faith, ask questions, and experience God's love for yourself.

Faith isn't about having all the answers or presenting a perfect life. It's about being open to taking one step at a time and trusting that God is walking alongside you, guiding and supporting you through every season. Whether you're beginning fresh or returning after a detour, God's invitation is always extended with compassion and hope.

If you feel ready to take that step today, or even if you're just curious, know that you are not alone. Countless others have started right where you are sometimes uncertain, sometimes hesitant, but always met with God's unfailing love. If you sense it's time to begin or renew your relationship with God, you can start with a simple prayer:

Prayer of Salvation (for those beginning their journey):

Father, in the name of Jesus,
I admit that I have made mistakes and lived for myself. I ask for Your forgiveness.
I believe that Jesus lived, died, and rose again for me. I give my life to You. Help me to live every day for You. I confess Jesus as my Lord and Savior.
Thank You for saving me. In Jesus' name, Amen.

If you prayed this prayer, take a moment to journal how you feel. What does this decision mean for your next chapter?

A Moment for Recommitment

Perhaps you once walked closely with God but now find yourself feeling distant, uncertain, or disconnected. Life has a way of pulling us in many directions, and sometimes our relationship with God can fade into the background. If that's where you find yourself today, know this: you are never too far gone. No mistake, detour, or season of doubt can separate you from God's love or disqualify you from His grace.

God's arms are always open, ready to welcome you back with unconditional love and acceptance. He delights in your return and desires to restore you, renew your spirit, and remind you of your purpose. This moment is an opportunity to lay down any burdens or regrets and embrace a fresh start, a new chapter in your walk with Him.

If you're ready to renew your commitment and draw close to God once again, you can begin with a heartfelt prayer:

Prayer of Recommitment:

Father, in the name of Jesus,
I ask You to create in me a pure heart and renew my spirit. Thank You for Your forgiveness and for never giving up on me. Help me to turn away from anything that separates me from You. Today is a new beginning. I recommit my life to You.
In Jesus' name, Amen.

If you prayed this prayer, take a moment to journal how you feel. What does this decision of recommitment mean for your next chapter?

Key Takeaways & Next Steps

As you close this journal, pause to remember the powerful truths and gifts God has placed before you. These are not just lessons to be learned but promises to be lived. Let them anchor you as you move forward:

1. **Knowledge for Your Journey:** God's Word is your guide, offering wisdom and direction no matter where you find yourself.
2. **Time and Patience to Grow:** Growth is a process, and God meets you with patience and grace at every step.
3. **Redemption and a Fresh Start:** Through Jesus, every day brings the possibility of new beginnings, free from the weight of your past.
4. **Complete Forgiveness:** God's forgiveness is total and unconditional — there is nothing you cannot bring to Him.
5. **A New Identity in Christ:** You are not defined by your mistakes, but by God's love and the new identity He gives you.
6. **Freedom to Live with Purpose:** No longer bound by fear or regret, you are free to pursue your calling and dreams with confidence.
7. **No Condemnation, Only Love and Guidance:** God's Spirit walks with you, offering encouragement, correction, and unwavering support.

Action Steps for Your Journey

Let these next steps serve as a practical guide as you continue to grow in faith and purpose:

Accept or recommit to Christ: If you feel led, take that step, whether for the first time or as a return. God meets you right where you are.

Engage with Scripture: Make the Bible a regular part of your routine. Let its truths inspire your writing, decisions, and heart.

Cultivate Prayer: Keep the conversation with God open. Invite Him into every area of your life, especially your creativity, challenges, and dreams.

Journal Your Journey: Capture your prayers, lessons, and breakthroughs. Reflection deepens your growth and helps you see God's hand in your story.

Celebrate Progress: No victory is too small. Celebrate each step, knowing that heaven rejoices with you (Luke 15:10).

Persevere: Growth takes time. Even small, steady steps move you forward, trust the process and keep going.

Final Reflection: Reaching the end of this workbook is not the end of your journey, it's a new beginning. As you continue to write, reflect, and pursue your calling, remember that you are seen, valued, and deeply loved. God's gifts are not just for a moment, but for a lifetime. Receive them fully, walk boldly in your purpose, and let these truths transform not only your writing, but every part of your life.

Take a moment now to reflect:

- What has changed for you through this process?
- How will you carry these gifts forward into your next chapter?

Remember, your journey is a masterpiece in progress. God is the loving Author, shaping your narrative, filling your days with meaning, and cheering you on as you grow into all He's called you to be.

Thank You

Your story and your calling matter. If you found encouragement, clarity, or inspiration in these pages, I invite you to keep growing with our community of faith-driven writers.

Visit www.drcharisrooks.com to discover:

- **Mentorship & Coaching:** Personalized guidance for Christian writers at every stage, from first idea to published book.
- **Publishing Programs:** Step-by-step support to help you write, publish, and even launch your own publishing imprint.
- **The Kingdom Writer Collection:** Books, journals, and resources designed to equip and inspire you to fulfill your divine writing mission.
- **Workshops & Digital Resources:** Practical tools, digital planners, and exclusive content to help you grow your writing, your brand, and your ministry.
- **Free 30-Day Social Media Planner:** Sign up for our mailing list and receive a complimentary planner packed with Christ-centered content strategies and a ready-to-use posting calendar.

You're not alone on this path. Let's walk together, so your words can reach, heal, and impact the world.

Connect, learn more, and take your next step at www.drcharisrooks.com.

Dr. Charis M. Rooks

Author

Meet the Author

Dr. Charis Rooks is an award-winning author and educator, specializing in graduate studies in business and ministry. She guides and supports doctoral candidates in the College of Divinity as a supervisor and proofreader for PhD and EdD students. As founder of Sapience Atelier Publishing Consulting and Inspired Grace Ministries, Dr. Rooks equips faith-driven writers to publish impactful books and build sustainable ministries. With an advanced degree in business leadership and a PhD in Christian Leadership and Ministry, she blends practical know-how with spiritual insight to empower others in their divine calling.

Proud mom to two daughters, nana to one amazing grandson, and devoted to her beloved dogs, both as a dog mom and "dog grandma," Dr. Rooks brings her signature warmth, wisdom, and inspiration to every book she writes. Her writing reflects her heartfelt desire to empower writers to pursue their calling and purpose, even in the face of life's toughest challenges. Dr. Rooks is currently continuing her theological studies at Rhema Bible Training College.

For more information, visit www.drcharisrooks.com.

Made in the USA
Coppell, TX
18 January 2026